GEOMETRY
of FIRE

GEOMETRY
of FIRE

Finding Peace After the Iraq War,
A Memoir

Paul Warmbier

atmosphere press

For Abbie, Simon, and Brooke
Who daily remind me where home is

CONTENTS

"I want to feel that I belong here, I want to hearken and know when I go back from the front line that the war will sink down, be drowned utterly in the great home-coming tide, know that it will then be past forever, and not gnaw us continually, that it will have none but an outward power over us."

— Erich Maria Remarque, *All Quiet on the Western Front*

"That is what I mean when I say that man is condemned to be free. Condemned, because he did not create himself, yet is nevertheless at liberty, and from the moment that he is thrown into this world he is responsible for everything he does."

— Jean-Paul Sartre, *Existentialism and Human Emotions*

ADDED WEIGHT

We wore degrees of brown and green. We stood in the full panoply of stained Nomex and Kevlar armor and steel dulled with electrical tape, both useful and ornamental, the bulk being unnecessary. When we patrolled, we begged for ways to lose the weight under the sun and melting asphalt. When we died, we died with or without all the weight.

We held and supported a scent of hope in the early days, which quickly dissipated into apathy, rage, and hopelessness coinciding immediately with the first death. It was a scent that welled up and hovered over our bodies. It was salty and malodorous, a ripeness the same as rotting fruit and as gritty as dead sluffed cells and old tears and clotted blood. Some never lost the scent, and it was often a prelude to the end. Above all, though, we carried sanity in a precarious grasp. We made the best of what we had. Once the idealism washed off us, we had to make meaning of the progressing entropy, and most of us could until we came home. For war is entropy, and when inside it, one can observe, but when home, memory removes the ability to chart changes easily.

Everyone carried the scent on him even after the armor came off. The brown and tan utilities were permanently caked with a thin line of white salt sweat around the chest like a target and a cut, deep into the flesh, though invisible. The line dried and crackled audibly while suiting up like river ice cracking before winter breakup. When the clothes came off, the scent of gunpowder and death and teenage command false bravado oozed out sickly sweet, molasses, and anger. It pooled around our tired feet and lay bubbling lazily in the heat.

The men of the heavy weapons platoon, "Gunfighters" we called ourselves, stood huddled in small groups, red skin under the red sun. We smoked in a circle and inhaled the unfiltered French cigarettes bought for three American dollars a carton, and the smoke became a deodorant, a mask, another facade. When we smoked, we joked – lewd, rough, fantasizing about sex, death, or both together. We joked about ways we would wash the scent off when the patrols ceased, of girls fucked, beers drunk, and risks taken where the bullets and hidden bombs no longer waited, perhaps one with our names on it. My name on it.

It was and still is only a matter of numbers and time, a lottery.

The lottery created meaning in each of us. We carried that meaning differently. For some, it became another curse. They waited to hurtle toward death. Some embraced it. Others, like me, attempted to accept the future, but let it seep in, handicapping mind and emotion. Constant death does that to people, regardless of the faux-righteousness of the struggle.

Each of the Kevlar-lined vests carried a discernible scent disproportional to age and experience. Billet.

Responsibility. The scent carried the names of dead comrades, and a mission to bring everyone home failed.

Few field units carried no extra weight, and all men flinched at the thump in the distance carrying the weight of iron and sour scent of explosive cordite and RDX. Burning almonds and smoke. Blood and screams. The final sour breath exhaled into crying faces clinging cheek to cheek as if physical touch was enough to save and return the pints of blood and pounds of flesh back to the bodies who used to own them.

That sour scent compounded and refused to wash off. The burden layered on, adding more weight. We were told we could remake the world through our service. We could make it better. Happier. More prosperous. Less corrupt. We all know how that turned out. I think we wanted to remake chaos. But order is hard to find and often lost in ego. All we made were nightmarish familial bonds.

I carried a letter in the folds of my armor. I remember the power in writing it. I didn't write many letters, and this may have been the only one I finished. I sat on the roof of our base all alone. I was on my cot and wrote with my paper on my knees. All night I wrote before getting it right. I burned the other copies in the same burn pit where we threw red sopping bandages with bits of flesh and bone clinging to them and old food and toxic batteries and bags of shit.

We knew where each other's letters were. We made silent pledges to retrieve them from our corpses if there was enough left for us to retrieve. We carried the certainty and inevitability with us everywhere. Life and death are random and death more so. I knew one moment we would be laughing, and the next watching blood seep from a sniper's bullet. We prepared for death by not letting it surprise us. I stopped thinking of life as an adventure, deployments as fun. I left that at home back in the States in order to be annihilated by war and remade into something entirely different.

We carried the burden of each other's lives. We brought the history of our deeds and fleeting hopes and dreams. We carried oaths sworn to save each other, die for each other. And like the scent, the weight of those burdens added up.

***

I built to get away. I made a shelter of trash and rubble to scramble into some shallow hole away from war and myself as the mortars tumbled down. It was foolish, honestly. I had a few tools and an insatiable desire to shut the door behind me, to me.

We built relationships to live and to hold each other up. Our experiences and upbringings were forgotten and replaced with shared suffering. We made deals with chiefs and Sheikhs and anyone else we could beg to help us defeat the enemy. The enemy. What was the enemy? Who were we trying to kill? Why were we building on some foundation that would be eroded the moment we smelled the whiff of freedom from the desert and someone else's war? Not my war anymore, man! The enemy really was weight and responsibility to each other, and some ideal we were told was patriotism.

I built a little shack twice in two deployments. Both were almost immediately destroyed. The first was in 2004 along a shimmering crystal bend of the Euphrates in north

Al Anbar, the diamond snake that made its way south and glittered as the immense desert sun reflected off it in waves. It's somehow true that the sun is larger and more stifling in the desert. It's not just the heat; it's the atoms and particles of light that impact and add weight to burden the invader. It's been that way since Gilgamesh and before nomads began settling down for the first time and before the desert took over the Arabian Peninsula.

When I built the first shelter along the banks, I had three materials: a sheet of plywood and two tent stakes. I created an angle against the sun that hid me from the oppression of light and gave me a sense of protection. It also allowed me to run away from my shelter quicker and hide on the berm of dust that protected us from the mortar rounds that fell incessantly and the rockets that floated over us like smoke-tailed kites to explode like iron fireworks that rained down on us.

I enjoyed building it, simple though it was. I enjoyed looking beyond its edges at night and seeing the full array of stars above me that are impossible to see anywhere near modern American cities. I enjoyed building it because I got to claim it as my own and rely on it, unreliable though it was. It collapsed once under the earthquake of outgoing mortars pounding into the earth like jackhammers feet away from my home. The ground thundered, and the concussive air bubble folded the tent stakes out from under, and they slid in the sand till I was sandwiched by the wood, still shaking as our mortar teams sent illumination and death skyward, the parachuting burst of light annihilating the night sky and my night sight. From then on, I slept on the wood instead of under it, my body armor my only blanket.

The second shack built over a year later was sturdy. About thirty kilometers south of Fallujah stood a small farm we occupied like so much else in that country. The compound consisted of three homes encircled by a cinder block wall topped with broken glass shards and razor wire that glittered like the river in the sun in the morning and evening as the light prismed through the shards. This one was framed with two-by-fours and closed off with plywood sheets. Three of us had racks. I built a monster bed frame out of spare pine left by the engineers, and I hammered in nails with a rock in both hands. Two weeks after moving into our new home, we were evicted by mortars once again.

In retrospect, I get it. The shack wouldn't have withstood a mortar round, and shrapnel would've splintered the frame, but at the time, I was furious. All my work was for naught.

I was furious a lot in those days.

There is no point building a home when its foundation is shaky, and the weight of hatred and fear bear down from all directions.

***

Three bullets ricocheted off an engine block. "The car refused to stop," we said, we pleaded to commanders, locals, ourselves. Three bullets, the recipe to stop a vehicle. Two shot off to the sun, leaving behind molecules of sparked iron and gasoline. The third ripped the kid's carotid artery to silky ribbons that fluttered momentarily like prayer flags high on a mountain sending thoughts and penitence off to the unknown. He couldn't have been more than fourteen. Another death among many. He lay there stinking of sweat and shit and American intervention.

Two of us sat up late that night, alone in the cold air, listening to cars beyond the wire, and the trash burn pit crackle as bags of shit were thrown into the flames to rain down on us in black soot. A sister squad of Marines lugged their vests and guns in the shadows to the staging area for a night ambush, their scent sour, unwashed, apathy wafting over in the cloud of burn-pit ash. "Why did it happen?" He repeated on a shaky loop like the end of a record as we sat listening to the night.

"It's war." That's all I could think of.

The textbook explanations were hollow and meaningless. They were true but withdrew none of the weight that was building and the burden that would never leave. The standard responses rarely are good enough. We sat. He talked. Recounting what happened over and over. I listened. How could I help? This was not my first fight, nor his. Not the first stray bullet. Not the last. With each one, it all burrowed deeper into the soul, harder to scrub away. It became us as our DNA replicated with a new mutation being encoded, now continuous, now the norm. It added a weight and indiscernible burden that eased with time but never fully peeled away.

Ever since this, I have tried to build the narrative of my war into something solid that I understand, but the rains always come up, and the wind always beats on my recreated world of memory, and it can never stand against fear and doubt. I have begun to try and make everything about me creation-focused. I think that if I can just generate something beautiful and perfect enough, the history of death that plagues me and wears me down can

9

be dispelled. The tough thing is that I know it can't. Once the weight piles on, it always seems to be there. The images, the pain, the death does not go away when the war zone is left behind because the war zone simply burrows down from the external to the internal. This is made especially hard when the external world is still a war zone of infighting about ideology and belief, and we see others bear down under the weight, and we want to help, but nothing ever seems to make a dent, to lift any burden.

That boy who crumbled under the weight of a torn artery and a mistake was nothing new. We always seem to build on shaky ground when we send boys and girls off to war to make them adults. This has been happening since the semi-mystical kings inscribed in the Sumerian King list attempted to take the sacred cities of Nippur and Ur and Uruk and the desert I knew, the whole of the cradle of us all, five thousand years ago and longer.

Political leaders have always appealed to the zeal and passion of youth to achieve their aims. And who does it benefit? It is almost impossible to relay to kids that what they are doing is nothing but a faulty system buried into the human genome that means war will be with us till our clocks stop. Our leaders seem to no longer even try to avoid war, but those who never fight continue to glamorize it while those who know what blood and guts smell like shake our collective heads and burrow into ourselves to remake meaning from the rubble. The boys and girls who wear the uniform briefly before being shoved with a pat on the back and false adulation into wars that have no reason or thought are destined to come home old, stooping, limping, and crying when they see what humanity is capable of. To say "it's war" is really to proclaim one of the absolute truths of humanity. "It's war" really means we're just human as we try to pass off our inability to lift the weight as an excuse. We are about to pass our failure to another generation already on shaky ground.

LETTERS
April 2009
Portland Oregon

Dear Family,

If you are getting this letter, I am dead. I wrote this because I do not want my last correspondence to be a five-minute phone call cut short by sniper fire or a letter asking about fixing my car. I have asked Mills to take the letter out of my flak jacket and mail it to you if I am killed.

Right now, it sits above my heart, protected by the ceramic plate. In a way, this letter is protection from death. It is an amulet. But as we say here, if your time is up, it's up.

It's all a lottery. And if my number is called, I am ready and have accepted it. I am in the company of the very best men on earth, and cannot imagine a better place to die.

I want you to know that I love you all. I joined the Marines to help and protect the weak, and despite the political bullshit, this war seems to me to be about helping the weak even if that is some unknown kid caught in the crossfire. I really feel that I am here to help these people, even if it is often so hard to do. I am proud of what I have accomplished, and I could not have asked for a more supportive and loving family throughout my short life.

If I die, know that you will all be on my mind to the last minute. Know also that if I die here, I die in faith, and will meet you once more, so it really isn't goodbye.

Love your son,

Paul

Is letter writing a dead art? Certainly, if you ask my grandparents, cursive is, to their dismay, but now, I think this may have been one of the letters I wrote and never sent during those years.

When I was in Iraq, letter writing was difficult. I had trouble sharing anything beyond the pleasantries of the day. How much should I write? Should I share the deaths and fears? The sights and smells? Or should I simply pretend all was ok, and that I was not going through inner torment as I slowly stopped believing in the moral power of America and the justness of the war?

When visiting my parents in Portland, Oregon, I often take the worn cedar stairs down past the innumerable spider webs, past the leftover paint, and cleaning solutions deep within the bowels of the house to the storage area. It sits secluded in the basement, hovering above the concrete like a little storm cloud of memories.

They live in a beautifully kept 1940's farmhouse, which is a relic of long past craftsmanship and is painted white except for a single plume of blue and red above the front door. It beckons guests with its display. It is perpetually washed clean by the reliable Oregon rain. The house is feet from the Lutheran church where my father is the pastor, and the proximity allows him to walk home every day, make his sandwich, and sit down heavily in front of the tv down in his man-cave to a few minutes of Monty Python or Hercule Poirot between counseling sessions, or writing the sermon for the next week, or sitting alone in the dark, high-ceilinged narthex tapping out next week's hymns on the piano. The old ivories have rested in an almost forgotten corner of the church, unmoved for decades. They are next to a glass case full of books showing off the history of the church in German ink and velum. Some of the keys are out of tune and tell a story slightly different than intended when pressed for answers. I love being in my parents' home and hearing the piano tinkle and tattle to the old hymns in the high-ceilinged narthex. They tell stories of human struggles and joy for hundreds and thousands of years. They remind us that we will all struggle, and that is life.

I love this house. I love the musty and mismatched red oak flooring that needs to be refinished in well-worn patches where guests have forgotten to remove their shoes. I love the hodgepodge of antiques my mother has accumulated and refinished over the years. The house is a home, and though it was never really my home, it is still a home.

My parents moved from the Idaho mountains near the Salmon River to Portland, Oregon after my senior year of High school and I lived there for only a month before shipping out to Marine Corps boot camp. The river-cut woods and sage foothills along the Bitterroots were my home, and to date, still seems to be one of the only places I feel truly comfortable. It is a home because it is comfortable, and there are memories, smiles, and laughter. It is a home because my letter is addressed to that house and would have been hand-delivered to my parents in case of my death probably long after uniformed officers holding a flag. The house is a home because now, the letters rest deep within, close to the furnace, never quite forgotten though packed deep down.

I grew up between northwest Montana and central Idaho. I was raised in an open green and tan country that seems only to exist in glossy photographs. My father taught me to pick out a hillside of elk grazing hundreds of yards above us, on some mountain almost above the tree line. He taught me to peer into gin-clear water where rocks shimmered like starlight and we would spot the thin undulations of trout swimming in the current. We would cast to those trout with long thin rods of graphite or fiberglass and our fly line would rest peacefully on the water before the fly was sipped off the surface and the thin line became a speckled cutthroat or brown trout in our hands.

In that place, animal tracks imprinted deeply in the thick bentonite mud, dust, and snow, and tracking was easy. The high mountain wind, always cool and crisp against my cheeks, even in August, is now nothing but a memory, another one in a house where memories line the walls and sit crowded in frames staring back at us from a time when I knew what *home* was. I killed my first animals in those hills in Idaho and watched the blood drip slowly from my shot into the grass and over the vibrant yellow wildflowers. Sometimes the bullets were not well placed because I was nervous or scared, and the blood seemed less like a trophy and more a crime.

It has always been secretly hard for me to kill anything and for a decade after my Marine service, I gave up hunting entirely, preferring to wade through baptismal water and cast at trout. As a kid, I never really was a killer who reveled in the killing, but one who did it because the freezer needed filling, or because even though it unsettles me, part of me enjoys being out and being a part of the circle of primal existence. Maybe that's what drew me to the Marines in the first place.

When I turned seventeen in 2002, I enlisted in the Marines. We still lived in Idaho at that time and the recruiters came to our house next to the church and for two hours talked to my parents at my behest trying to get them to understand the adventure I was called to go on.

After, on deployment, wherever I tried to call home, I searched in my parent's voices for the same hint of mountains or a tree line or a whisper of cool wind I could recognize, but my memory was sharply blurred by heat waves rising from the asphalt as my feet plodded one after the other in the sand.

Bullets zipped through the heat waves breaking up my memory of where home might be. Trash hid cylinders of iron, nitro-glycerin propellant, and RDX high explosive. People hid explosives in their clothes and would smile and wave before evaporating into smoke and iron shards. At first, I waved back but that didn't last. Eventually, I stopped waving at the kids and would instead raise my weapon, drawing a cross on them through the scope with the intent to scare the little kids away. I had learned what kindness gave us.

For years, I could not find anything I could call home, and when on leave, the cityscape of Portland provided a new environment devoid of rocky streams and elk and everything else I craved. It was also devoid of zipping bullets and chemicals exploding outwards at three thousand feet per second and of blood. I could not just come home like my parents asked. I didn't know where home was.

Here is the central question of my life post-war: Is it possible to come *home* and stop my existential wanderings?

Many Marines I have talked to hint at some inability they feel. Many feel restless and nervous. Almost like they are traveling on some path, and the trail disappears into a mire of thickets and alternative trails.

Descending my parent's staircase is a bit like going back into time. Once in the concrete basement, I navigated the two rooms stealthily. The basement is lined floor to ceiling with camping gear, kids' books waiting sad and alone in bins for my siblings and me to have babies grow to readers, an antique train set from my late grandpa—that now sits in a circle around my office coffee table next to a conductor's hat that my son wears—and other artifacts from my youth.

Even in the basement, I cannot get away from antiques and memories of what home used to feel like. Somewhere buried deep is a box titled simply "Paul." I always would stop here and slowly rifle through it. I don't know why I always have to look through it. I know what it contains. It is a mirror into my past. It is loaded with crap I didn't care to take to my new life. However, in the depths is something more.

My box is a safe. One of discarded Marine

paraphernalia, a child's blanket—carefully knitted by my grandmother before I was born, it still is stained in places, waiting to be washed—several books mostly of the adolescent type, cassette tapes of my favorite artists, and mixes I made (probably illegally) from the weekly "Casey Kasem American Top 40" broadcast, Random CDs from video games and artists I couldn't play anymore, and down at the bottom, in a brown and brittle envelope, are my letters from my enlistment.

I take them out. Gingerly. I smile despite myself as I relive those experiences. I wonder where the letters from my deployments were. I have seen everything in the box before, why have I not noticed letters from deployment? I put the lid back on and sit on the tub, thinking. *Surely, I wrote home on my deployments.* "Hey, Mom!" I yell upward through the delicate patina of spider's webs clinging to cedar floor joists.

"What, honey?" She answers right above me. It sounds like she is preoccupied, probably reading a magazine, probably about refinishing furniture or quilting. Probably in that chair surrounded by family photos. There is one of me in the mix on my second deployment. I felt her feet beat a ragged tattoo on cedar above. It reverberated down, an omen.

"Did I send letters home from deployment?" Silence. Maybe she didn't hear me. I move forward in history, leaving my own on the floor. Upstairs in the living room, I ask again. Silence. She looks at me a little sad.

"No, you did not send any home at all. However, I know we sent many to you. Wait, you sent one. Just one." She looks back to her magazine (it was a furniture magazine).

"Sorry, I guess you're right. But I did try to call about once a month."

"Once a month. Yes, those occasional calls were nice."

"Can I see the one I sent?"

Here is the deal. I feel bad for not writing home, but what was I supposed to write home about? I remember starting letters and getting only about three lines into them.

Hey Mom and Dad,

I hope everything there is great. I am fine. It really is hot here.

Where do I go from there? How on earth am I supposed to tell them the truth? I was in the Al Anbar province of Iraq. I was in Fallujah, Hit, Haditha, and Rawaa. I was in a world of prehistory and mystique and terrible beauty.

How was I supposed to skip the bad stuff? It just didn't seem right at the time to talk to them about mortar attacks, RPGs, wounded men, pools of blood that would not filter through the sand, and charred bodies that resembled carbonized firewood cracked with jagged lines of pink where the meat and fat showed through.

Once a few days after an attack that put five of my brothers into an airplane headed for Germany, I sat down with the chaplain. He came around once or twice a month. He was Baptist, but I could handle it. Lutherans like me are grumpy and are not demonstrative in church. I wasn't sure about a Baptist, but he was all I had. He was a small man with a little mustache. It was pencil-thin, and I could never help looking right at it. His cammies, clean, hung off his little frame. I always thought he was pretending to be a soldier in that way little kids do with their parent's hand-me-downs. If it were not for his mustache, I would have thought him an impostor.

After the blood and flesh finally congealed and sank into the sand, we talked. I hadn't been sleeping much. "Sir, I don't know what to do. I can't stop dreaming about it. I can't stop being pissed all the time. I want to kill all these fuckin' people here."

"Have you thought about prayer?" the scope of the question was at odds with the smallness of his hands. They were light, moisturized, and minuscule. They jumped from place to place when he talked. His words seemed calm, but his hands had ADD. I couldn't focus on anything else besides the hands and that mustache. They were untrustworthy, I thought. They were green and rarely left the comforts of the base.

I gawked. "Seriously, sir, you think I haven't thought about praying? Praying is all I have been doing this whole deployment. Praying the snipers would stop, praying I could just go home, praying my girlfriend isn't screwing someone else, praying we don't get hit by the next fucking IED, Christ sir!" I took a deep breath. He just sat there looking at the dirt. "Sorry, sir."

"I understand your frustration, son. Prayer doesn't always work, I know. Have you thought about writing home?"

I was done. He was trying. But I was out of patience and this was eating into my limited rest time. The time I could use smoking a dry cigar that I knew would make me sick, or time laying on a cot on the roof of our house, out in the sun, shirt and pants off, nothing but me and the heat and the sun and the fractious homelessness of my mind.

Sitting on my rack under the building's only air conditioning unit, I grabbed my body armor and reached deep into the front pouch behind my armor plate. In a plastic baggie, I found the envelope. It was still ok. I did not open the sealed paper; to do so, it seemed, would be an invitation. It was my death note. One is wise to not re-read their own death note too often.

I resealed the plastic and put it back in my flak over my heart. It wasn't a long or deeply poetic letter as death letters seem to always be in literature. But I felt it was honest, and that was enough.

I took out another piece of paper and addressed it to my dad.

Dear Dad,

Am I going to hell if I kill anyone? What if I really want to, I mean, really want to, or need to? Can I ever be me? Can I ever go home, you know, really?

I closed the pad of paper and walked away from it. I never finished or sent the letter. I never sent any letter but waited for my next turn with the satellite phone.

I remembered a conversation I had with my dad after my first deployment in 2004. It was sometime around Christmas and was yet another Christmas I was just not in the spirit. I knew I was going back, and even then, was troubled with desires to kill. My good Lutheran upbringing told me that killing was a mortal sin, but what about with the soldier? What are we to do?

"You know, every time we turned on the TV, we looked for you." My father mentioned looking up from his ham sandwich a few days into one visit after talking to my mom. "We really didn't want to watch it, but the possibility we would see you was hard to ignore, no matter how slim the chance." I just looked at my sandwich and didn't really eat.

"Sorry I didn't write much." He didn't mean to, but somehow I already felt ashamed for my inability to write home. How could I write about the deployment in terms that both my parents could get? I know they wanted none of the fear of IEDs, the understanding that the ground underneath could collapse in fire and smoke, the acid perfume filling the blast area, our mouths, and the dust settling on exposed skin, making us premature ghosts. "Dad, to be honest," I blurted out what I tried to say for days. "I really just didn't know what to say that wasn't bad. I knew I couldn't write to mom about *it*."

"Have you ever read Luther's letter to Von Kram?" this caught me off guard, and I struggled to fit how this related to anything.

"No. What was it about?" My dad, a master of obscure and strangely poignant theological knowledge, reached the real issue.

"I heard that you went to church when you were on base." My godfather, a Navy chaplain, now the Chaplain of the Coast Guard, deployed to Afghanistan around the time I deployed to Iraq, and he monitored me through the chaplain network. It surprised me how much my dad really knew.

"I went a few times; our chaplain was an ok guy. What does this have to do with Luther?"

"Well, Asa Von Kram was a nobleman and knight during the reformation. He struggled with the moral implications of being both a Christian and a soldier." My father sometimes adopted a low staccato rhythm when teaching. This made listening enjoyable and contained a *gravitas* that was hard to ignore. I have attempted, largely unconsciously to mimic it in my own teaching. "He talked to Luther and said it was hard to reconcile how killing fit into the Christian confessions. He just didn't see how it was possible to kill and know he could still go to heaven. Or be a good person."

"How did Luther untangle the problem?"

He explained that the role of the soldier, as Luther says, is twofold. First, they are there to ensure the punishment of the wrong and the protection of the good. If there is a misuse of the military, it doesn't invalidate the field or the need for it, but just requires the individual to act judiciously on his own to execute the potential *good* in the given order.

"And this has to do with me not writing home how?"

"I know that you, at times, had to act in a way that makes it hard to be a person in this world where normalcy is needed, and anything out of the ordinary is condemned. I know you struggle now; I see it." He looked me straight in the face. "But that does not mean that you can never come back as yourself. You can use the change in a good way. You chose to not correspond with us because you did not want to correspond with yourself."

On my last night on base south of Fallujah in 2005, I took the death letter out of my flak jacket, gingerly removed it from the plastic, and without opening it, tossed it into the flames of our campfire.

A START

I once heard that to get a fresh start in life, one must go very far and could never come back home. By the summer of 2003, I not only was ready to run away from the small town I was raised in, but I knew that if I did not leave forever, I would not leave at all. That's the kind of town Salmon, Idaho, was. When you left, you left for good, or like swimming in a vortex, no strength of volition would ever allow change. It took me many years to get to that point. My life began in the privilege that small-town kids of middle-class families all had, namely, an expectation of college, success, a job, homeownership, and happiness.

I was born late August 1985 while the crickets cackled their mating displays one to another in a length of never-ending radio static. Whitefish, Montana had not yet reached its boom point as a haven for skiers, and the dual parish Lutheran churches my father ministered to allowed us to live in nearby Columbia Falls. It was a mill town on the tracks of the Great Northern Railway whose freight and passenger cars rumbled through the Mission Mountains.

Columbia Falls always seemed to be trying to decide

whether it preferred mill, locomotive, or cigarette smoke. Mostly, it invited all three. In the mid to late eighties, loggers and Glacier Park cowboys patrolled the numerous bars at night red flannels with perpetually rolled sleeves thin and see-through with age and weeks in the saddle and under the sun, and tin cloth pants, and stained Stetsons slowly breaking down like iron coated in rust, always hopelessly torn and stained provided the town with a classic Montana cliché that seems to be gone these days. For better or worse.

These days, I love that cliché and try to live up to it as some kind of grumpy birthright, but somehow can never quite manage. I think I was too privileged to rise to that world. I was never tough enough to be a real logger, and never outside enough, and willing to accept privation stoically to be a cowboy even though I have often gone through the motions of both of those jobs. Perhaps because I was never really a cowboy, and knew I never would be, and perhaps because I never really wanted to be a cowboy. My uncle was. When he was a kid, Uncle John or UJ, was a cowboy in the park and rode uncounted miles of trail. I looked up to him and his wildness and wanted to make it my own.

I would see those long-lost tough men with awe and wonder as their boots hit hard on the concrete and jingled like it was Christmas with each step. I read Louis L'amore books and had a cowboy hat and bucked bales, worked cattle, rode horses to round 'em up, avidly paid attention to rodeos, and rode fences all through high school. But knowing that was not my life, eventually, the awe would redirect to another closer to home: the military.

I was born into an intellectual light patch in the smoke and flannel. With my father being a Lutheran pastor, he and my mother were unusually educated for both the time and place. He had just finished his Masters of Divinity a year or so before I showed up, and my mother was a schoolteacher fresh from her first teaching job: the kids in south St. Louis, where my father was going to the Seminary. He had a library more diverse than the town's selection. What's more, he expected all his kids to be just as well read.

One of the first real books I remember reading was an adaptation of Homer's *Iliad and Odyssey*. The lines of epic verse pushed into corners where pictures of Achilles surrounded by his Myrmidons stormed the plains of Troy ahead of a thousand ships' sails painted into the blue distance and melancholy visions of Prince Hector kissing his newborn child goodbye for the last time. The hope of conquest or defense on their lips, and even though I knew it to be a silly ambition, those images stood guard over my imagination.

My father woke early each day, sometimes around 4:30 or 5, and read his small blue bible written in Greek script. I looked through it at times when he left it out. I couldn't read it, obviously, but loved looking through the archaic scratches of ancient writing. Each page was filled with a small thin hand explaining in English how some word was conjugated or the meaning shift from early to late Greek, then Latin. He alternated that with Latin and Hebrew scholarship, the early church fathers, patristics, and Christian philosophy. Augustine, Origen, Luther, C.S. Walther, and others coming alive in his mind before he carefully put the book down as my sister and I made the noises of waking up which echoed through the small ranch house. He would help get us dressed and fed, and then he'd meander off to the church office to prepare for each day's activities: bible study, meeting with other pastors, house calls with shut-in parishioners, planning for Sunday's sermons, writing theological essays, or counseling. From what I am told, we had little extra money each month and the excess would turn into books. We had all we could read and more.

I was also born into a military family. Long before my dad took a call to another small parish in central Idaho when I was around eight, I knew where I was going to go in life. My grandfather—my mom's dad—was a decorated soldier in the Korean War, and whispers of his struggles and fights wafted their way—fought through, really—the English pipe tobacco and sour cheap beer on his breath as he drank himself into coherence at night. His large six-foot-two or three frame topped with stark white crew-cut hair maintained good discipline and order alongside his army issue boots. These stood testament to the legacy of the Frozen Chosen, the survivors of the Pusan, and those battered to bits under the guns on Pork Chop Hill. I never once heard his war stories but instead saw his body and soul as a totem that told me all I needed to know about his life in the military.

Walt let his guard down only a few times when I was a kid. Usually, it was when he was drunk and kind—for Walt was only ever a kind and loving drunk. A few pints of Milwaukee's best seemed to let him shed his anger and PTSD and become the loving grandfather he always seemed to want to be. I knew the military was my way, there was no question about it.

Once, I put on a rice paddy hat made for river rafters. I felt a jerk on my arm and turning, saw his old and thick finger almost poke me in my eye while the other hand jerked off the hat. "If you ever wear one of those again, I'll kill you." He hissed so no one could hear but me. I smashed the hat back down on the shelf hastily, like touching it was poison I didn't know was there.

He didn't look at me the rest of the day until we got home, and he retired to my dad's workshop, and I went outside and wandered around with a stick. Eventually, I wound my way into the shop to grab something and Walt was sitting there with my dad chatting and smiling amiably. Perhaps they were discussing the church or Christianity—Walt was an impassioned biblical scholar in his own right—Walt called me over and had me climb up onto his lap. I was hesitant, but his thin arms enveloped me, and I felt his scratchy beard stubble and the smell of cold pipe tobacco and it seemed all was forgotten, and he just wanted to be a grandpa. All I wanted was for him to be a grandpa too, but when he sat and stared off in the distance, I now know that he was back in Korea. I do the same when I am reminded of Iraq and hope that I do not grab my son's arm when he does something odd.

We moved to Idaho from Montana. Sometime in the early nineties we wound our way south through a mountain pass and along a trout-filled river to the Lemhi valley and Salmon, a tiny blip on the map surrounded by great mountain ranges, high deserts and passes that nearly killed Lewis and Clark when they came through. In Idaho,

I was raised to be self-sufficient and independent along the foothills of the Bitterroot range. I learned to find my direction in the thick forests by the sun and the land. I learned some truth to the world through the wilderness and in the rivers and lakes formed by the draining of the Great Missoula Floods millennia prior. Over all those years, I imagined the same small starlings chirping and bouncing from aspen and cottonwood branches along the ever-flowing river banks, the same ungulates changing only due to adaptation and the number of predators stalking the mountains. I was always a visitor. I rarely have felt otherwise.

My father took my brother, Matthew—two years younger than I—and myself up into the mountains with fishing rods and knives and hatchets and hunting rifles to learn the essentials of living and observing. Those years were indispensable to me and my growth into a person able to wander the deserts of California and Iraq to train and operate against an unknown enemy who was better at living out in the wilderness than us. Those years were also crucial for an understanding of who I was deep down where I thought war couldn't touch me.

As I grew and decided on my path, the choice of the Marine Corps was a bit much for my parents to swallow—particularly after 9/11—but on my seventeenth birthday, I drove the windy high mountain roads from Salmon, Idaho to Boise with my recruiter to enlist. There were only two of us in the transport van built for fourteen. I sat in the second-row middle seat and pretended to not be sick with nerves and homesickness and the windy road. He drove at minimum twenty miles an hour over the limit and took hairpin mountain turns at fifty. I was going to sign a promise to live in the fast lane for four years, and my wild eyes glued themselves to the road as I tried to keep lunch down.

My recruiter was the first real Marine I ever saw. He was short and stood erect in that way that all strong, wiry kids did who were confident of their strength among lessers. It was a confidence I lacked and a posture I tried to emulate even as I failed. He had been an infantryman, an assault man specializing in anti-armor and demolitions. He told stories of wargames and nights spent huddled in foxholes in Australia, Korea, The Republic of Georgia, anywhere where war wasn't taking place, but training for some unknown future war was needed. I sat passively in the car, my stomach churning only partly from the car trip, trying not to ask the questions that swirled around my head and I begged time to speed out of control so I could understand what he meant, what my grandfather meant when he mumbled late at night after dinner.

When we moved from Montana to Idaho, I exchanged quiet drives through Glacier park with Sunday drives into the indomitable Sawtooth and Bitterroot Ranges looking for the multitude of ghost towns and the occasional mine that reminded us of the boom and bust history of the West. The drives were not times to force us into the paths of rattlesnakes and bears, or to glass elk two and three ridges over with my dad's worn and paint chipped spotting scope; they were instead refreshing transcendental experiments. They stood as brief moments of understanding into the world and its hostility. "Paul,

Spud!" (My brother's nickname since birth has always been Spud.) My dad would occasionally whisper those words excitedly while pointing half a mile away on some barren brown mountain scree slide to a black bear, elk, or mule deer. He would always whisper as if the volume and frequency of normal speech would break the spell holding all parties involved where we were.

Several years later, and four or five deer seasons into my teenage years, I stood above, watched, and waited. I sunk deep in the snow while listening to the wind whistle in my ears moving over the ridgeline like a wave. I rested my 30-06's slight and delicate walnut stock in the snow scratching it on a protruding pine branch mostly submerged in a drift. My eye found the relief in the reticle, and a four-point buck stood with two does looking considerably closer than reality and quartered by a thin crosshair. I had a choice. This was late in the season, and I knew unless I stumbled on another deer the same day, I'd lose my opportunity for a kill that year and forfeit meat in the freezer. I tried to control my breath and force a smooth inhale and exhale as I debated the shot.

The range was a little long, roughly four hundred yards, but I thought I was sure to make it. That was the year I signed the papers that would set me on the path, and I was aware I would exchange shooting deer for people. I was excited about it at that time as odd as that sounds. I wanted to prove myself, my masculinity, my toughness. I had always thought men in the West did not prove themselves through poetry or emotion but killing and action. I tended towards poetry but wanted to be still accepted. I was willing to do anything. I breathed slowly, waiting for the deer to turn perpendicular to me.

Slowly, minute by minute, he turned, and I squeezed the trigger in minute increments. The rifle rocked back in my arms. My eyes closed as the report echoed loud through the snow-covered valley. He dropped. The bullet was high, and when the gun settled back, I saw the shot broke his back paralyzing him and his neck thrashed in a rainbow of low arcs in the white snow, flecks of red staining the blanket of white while his back legs rested almost calm like he was sleeping.

I ran through the waist-deep snow and soon stood over him while his eyes stared, unfixing, at me. I just stood and stared back for minutes. I pulled out my long knife my other grandpa gave me. I slit his throat inexpertly, and it took me several strokes before he spurted red, the blood drained out of my body just as it did his. The weight of life for the first time ever hit me, and I remember sitting in bloody snow with crimson hands and pants, and my smile turned to tears as we watched each other, him dying, me washing myself of innocence.

Our house in Idaho was out of town to the west a mile or two and on five acres of land. The highway we lived along was the old railroad line from Idaho Falls to Salmon, and the road was an unbroken brush stroke punctuated with big wide sweeping turns that arched out of sight behind mountain ranges. It was easy to imagine being on a train while driving that road and looking out the windows at the rugged and unforgiving mountains to the north and south.

For a kid with a wild imagination, this was the place of dreams. I spent summers experimenting with firecrackers stuck in the mud, and winters experimenting with others stuck in ice. I kicked boulders down mountainsides and jumped in puddles in the road that ran by our house and fed the horses that soon knew all of my siblings and me by sight. I played in a treehouse nestled in the knee of an ancient cherry tree where the pits gathered at the base like ball bearings. Breaking, exploding, and ruining things were my past times, and I was quite good at them. Once I found a machete and spent the better part of a whole summer chopping my parent's innocent garden plants to shreds, not to mention the unsuspecting fence posts and log pile.

The landscape was special. It was the kind of sagebrush and pine hills only usually seen in western movies. From my old house looking north, the low hills wrapped up the mountains in a blanket that led to foothills of thick pine and further up, rock and snow. The Bitteroots are the border between Montana and Idaho and extend to the end of sight to the southeast and the meeting of the Sawtooths to the northwest. Where the two ranges meet, the Salmon river rushes through, squeezed between the two layers of granite and slowly eating its way through a canyon. Lewis and Clark made their way through that canyon in 1805 unprepared for the barrier the river and rock would become. As I grew, I became part of the stone and wood, soil, and air unique to Idaho. When I left, I would carry that with me to the Middle East and it would act as a bulwark to the changes in me.

When not destroying my parent's possessions, I spent hours in the hills and on the slopes of the Bitterroots, single-shot shotgun or fly rod in hand. In the ten years, we lived there, I probably existed inside only a fifth of the time.

***

I took my driving test at fifteen. I failed the first time, but the officer conducting my written test said she would look the other way and let me pass. It could have been my pleading smile, or the tears welling up. Either way, I got my license. My first car was a 1980 Toyota pickup, the precursor to the Tacoma. It cost four hundred and sixty-four dollars and got about four miles to the gallon. We bought it from some of my father's parishioners when I was fifteen. It was a stick shift, and I proceeded to almost drive it into the side of our church within minutes of getting it home. The truck was tan and pockmarked with dents, and I drove that little pickup high into the mountains, rattling over roads many Jeeps would not have tried. I carried a portable CD player with external speakers because the radio in the truck didn't work. Driving over the mountain roads, anthems from my high school years skipped their way along; Bad Religion, Billy Joel, AFI, and the Sex Pistols accompanied me drowning out birds and squirrels. When the truck inevitably got stuck, my friends and I got out and pushed. When I was alone, I walked to farmhouses, or down the hills and waded across the often-frozen Lemhi river to ask if Dad could bring his truck and tow me home. I led a life of ease and wonder where each rock and tree was another prop to some illusion. Salmon didn't seem to be the real world until some national tragedy brought us closer to the rest of the states.

BOOT CAMP
Summer 2003

My story actually begins here. It seems all war narratives start here. In *All Quiet on the Western Front,* the seminal anti-war narrative of World War One, Paul Baumer and his friends are shown muddied, abused, and miserable in training. Boot camp for the Marine is full of physical and verbal abuse, mud, sand, blood, and pain.

In boot camp, one is of little more value than slug shit. Recruits stay for just a week in a receiving platoon doing such asinine activities as standing in long lines staring straight ahead for hours. They donate an unhealthy and astounding volume of blood for tests and god knows what other diabolical needs. They receive vaccinations *en masse,* turn and cough for yet another exam requiring some old man—who most likely conceals a lineage with the SS—to finger shriveled balls for a disconcertingly protracted amount of time. All is endured with a mixed bag of fear, worry, and eventual cowed relief when the sound of a snapping glove and dejected sigh tell us we are good to go.

We pass a long time in an empty room waiting,

knowing they will somehow find out if we'd lied to them, in order to pretend that no, you have never smoked pot, not even once— *wait, does it count if I never inhaled? What if I just held the bong for a friend? Does a contact high count?* We stand still for hours, the drill instructors bouncing around us like angry dogs on leashes just long enough to scare you but also to keep your face from being eaten.

The recruits march together to Black Friday—which unfortunately has nothing to do with after Thanksgiving sales at Wal-Mart—the shaking fear the darting eyes, and reevaluation of life's choices similar to what I imagine BASE jumping for the first time is like.

On this day, the recruit meets his drill instructors. They are always hulking gentlemen perfectly dressed from cover to shoes with no blemish anywhere. The attention to detail is staggering. When going to school to become a drill instructor, hours each day are spent focusing specifically on the attention to detail needed to turn kids into killers.

I joined my other recruits in a large squad bay big enough for one hundred bunk beds spaced along either wall. I stared ahead, not out of discipline but fear, my drill instructors' hard and pinched faces staring back. My hands shook slightly, I clenched them into fists to stop. Around me, my fellow recruits, pants unbloused (meaning not tucked-in), no camouflage overshirt, just a stark white undershirt tucked into pants, we looked decidedly not like Marines. Each aspect of the uniform is earned. We were then what recruits further along in the process would call "Heinous" and "Nasty turds." We had to earn not being that.

Phase one began with a day of introductions. The instructors introduced themselves as Sergeant Johnson, Sergeant Miller, and our senior drill instructor, Staff Sergeant Walker. Miller and Johnson turned to Walker, and in a low growl, he gave them command of us. "Sergeants, take command, and execute the order of the day."

"Aye, aye, Sir." Then Sgt. Walker left. The other two exploded with orders, "Get your sorry asses in front of a rack right now! Ten, nine, eightsevensixfivefourthree-twoonnneee, and you are done!" He screamed the last word and it hit like an ocean-born gale. "Stop where you are, you sons of bitches!" they shot back and forth down the line physically placing people where they should be with the soles of their boots and the palms of their hands. Luckily, I was fast and had a rack, but saw someone kicked and they skidded a short distance on waxed concrete in front of another bunk bed. My hands were really shaking now. After every incoherent shouted order, there was a pause followed by a "Do you understand!?" we replied, "Yes, Sir" at the top of our lungs. We usually had to repeat the two words five to ten times because somehow, we didn't yell loud enough.

The instructors had us running back and forth all day; they themselves were shortly hoarse and soaked head to toe in sweat. During a break, Johnson retreated to a small room where the three of them kept an office and came back almost instantaneously with a fresh uniform. For the next several weeks, we screamed ourselves mute, ran or marched everywhere, and even at night stayed terrified, for late at night, the instructors withdrew from their huts to sneak around, terrify the guards, and walk by our exhausted heads to whisper threats.

Boot camp is not so much a test of physical prowess as a series of up games, gauntlets, and tests designed to break us from kids dreaming about mountains to Marines who dreamt about war. I ran cross-country in middle and high school as well as being a moderately decent sprinter. I had no problem with the physical aspect of boot camp. I also had enough pent-up aggression that fighting came easy. Even if I was no good at it. I got my ass kicked each time I was on the Pugle sticks or learning MCMAP (The USMC Martial Arts program).

PFTs were given regularly—consisting of a five-kilometer run, pull-ups, and sit-ups—I normally could max out or almost max out the requirements of an eighteen-minute three-mile run, twenty pull-ups and one hundred sit-ups in two minutes.

What really was the focus in boot camp was mental toughness and, by extension, discipline. Training for discipline consisted partially of standing stock still for hours in rain, heat, and cold, everything and in the precise, calculated movements of close-order drill. The trick was to forget about everything around you and go brain dead to thinking. All that mattered was instantaneous processing, an automaton's progression through algorithms pre-programed through repetition.

Discipline was about forgetting pain and discomfort. It was about getting in the fighting ring and moving until there was nothing left. Discipline built an instant willingness to comply with orders regardless of personal safety. Marine discipline is a hardening of the mind and body for whatever may come. It is an unfeeling under-standing that when it matters, we are not individuals, we act as a single unit, we are machine men.

Phases two till the end were all about the transition from fear and pain to indoctrination and mentorship. The goal was to change us from kids to men and women who thought differently, spoke differently, and responded to situations in a precise and well-mechanized motion. Later, training in individual combat would become a focus, but in boot camp, it was all about being a machine. *That* is what makes Marines so formidable. From day one, the mental beating breaks the recruit down and rebuilds the mind and body into a single fighting unit. I am convinced no other military boot camp in the world offers such a comprehensive and holistic indoctrination.

The military thought it a good idea long ago to rename all objects that make little sense at all. For example, why would a rational mind change the name from the toilet to the head? Why do windows have to be portholes, the floor a deck? Or, why call a drinking fountain *and* a juicy rumor, scuttlebutt? (The last is a personal favorite)

We learned these new names quickly and within hours, started using them excessively, and with a little bravado during the hour of free time at night before bed. We began to strut, thinking we knew something unique and special. We started thinking and responding in this manner.

We were in an abusive relationship.

I reached out one day in the second phase with shaky

and nervous hands, receiving my weapon. I learned to assemble and disassemble the black cold steel of the M-16 rifles. Every part of this weapon looked designed to kill efficiently. The weapon is heavy, around eight pounds, and the weight minimizes recoil. I was always amazed how, when on the range, or later in Iraq, I could shoot, and almost immediately regain the target in my sight. And when my adrenaline would boil, I remember no recoil at all, no movement of the sight, just the movement of my finger and the glow of the tracers. The barrel was a thick cylinder that helped keep the weapon cool, maximizing accuracy at ranges of up to seven or eight football fields. The round, 5.56 millimeters in diameter, or caliber, when fired, exploded out of the barrel at supersonic speeds. The small round, when impacting a person, was designed in such a way so it slows down in moments and bounces around in the target's body, rupturing organs. My fellow recruits and I entrusted with this killing weapon knew every aspect of it in a matter of weeks.

I was around eight or nine when I shot my first gun. My dad trained my brother and me on an old bolt action .22 and revolver. Each shot mattered. He taught us that when hunting, the animal ideally collapses under the impact of one single well-placed round behind the front shoulders, shredding the lungs, and perforating the heart. Death was quick, it was as humane as possible, and most importantly, it put meat in an otherwise empty freezer his pastor's salary struggled to maintain.

My father imparted a reverence of guns and weapons of every sort. They were not feared, as they were simple tools of wood and steel, but were revered as tools entrusted to us for one purpose alone. That being said, I have never been an expert shot. As a kid, I lacked patience for well-placed shots at extreme distances. My brother and father always beat me when we took the bolt action out and played war with GI Joes, lining them up and shooting at them.

In the early nineties, Mattel, or some other company made over-sized plastic molded GI Joes and they became our targets. One green warrior, who stood all of six inches on his base forever, attempted to throw a grenade that wouldn't have left his hand anyway, and another tried to immolate his enemies with a green flame thrower, and there was an officer, beckoning his men forward into the breach. He usually died first, but we killed them all. We scraped away the plastic exit wound with a knife before lining them up for another turn. At twenty or thirty yards, they proved quite the targets as they hid in the grasses and advanced over the open field. The game was to have five enemies, and six rounds. The shooter was limited to a one-minute turn and attempted to kill all the green bastards.

We recruits memorized and began to understand the rules of law and the intent behind the Uniform Code of Military Justice. I learned the eleven general orders before the whole of the Uniform Code of Military Justice.

Let's learn all the ways that you can fuck up and be put into the brig or even worse, CCU.

On a quick sidetrack, CCU or the correctional custody unit is a cool idea. I saw these poor turds at work in Pendleton. They go out to a stone quarry in the morning and turn big rocks into smaller rocks all day with a six-pound sledge and so repeat until their sentence is over. It's a bit draconian, but I hear it works.

From these rules, all judicial and wartime decisions are supposed to derive. There are 11 General Orders that govern almost every facet of duty.

1. To take charge of this post and all government property in view.

2. To walk my post in a military manner, keeping always on the alert and observing everything that takes place within sight or hearing.

3. To report all violations of orders I am instructed to enforce.

4. To repeat all calls from posts more distant from the guardhouse than my own.

5. To quit my post only when properly relieved.

6. To receive, obey, and pass on to the sentry who relieves me, all orders from the commanding officer, officer of the day, and officers and noncommissioned officers of the guard only.

7. To talk to no one except in line of duty.

8. To give the alarm in case of fire or disorder.

9. To call the corporal of the guard in any case not covered by instructions.

10. To salute all officers and all colors and standards not cased.

11. To be especially watchful at night and, during the time for challenging, to challenge all persons on or near my post and to allow no one to pass without proper authority.

Knowing them front to back, meant not thinking about the right decision while on duty. Any thought of ethical conundrum while on duty was included in our rules.

Discipline begins to take form in phase two, and if you are not forced to learn how to ruin your career or are being worked out until you vomit all over the back of another recruit in front of you, the platoons are on the blacktop learning drill.

Zero nine-hundred hours, the drill instructors called for every swinging dick to meet on the parade deck just outside of the squad bay. I forget what we were doing, but it was most likely learning how someone fucked up earlier that morning while waiting in line for chow. There was always something out of line that caused us recruits to suffer. There was always someone who could not meet the time constraints to ordinary tasks. Ten, nine, eight. After ten, the countdown sped up until the instructor sounded like an experienced auctioneer. Staff Sgt. Walker always slowed down perceptibly at around the count of two or three and ended on a long and drawn out bark of "And you're done!" this morning, most likely, someone still was out of line by the ending of the countdown heralded their doom. I like to imagine their eyes turned from concentration to a frantic frenzy around three, and their hands started shaking, making any progress impossible. Chances are, they gave up and gave in to the inevitable.

We lined up for drill in long-practiced places. I was directly behind the third squad leader, a small man with little dark eyes whose menacing, beady glares that told me if I was one step out of line, he would tattle. Staff Sgt. Walker slowly limbered his fatherly frame out the door as the last recruit followed. In a deep bark Walker bellowed, "platoon, count, off!" and we counted several times. This time, the guy who messed up in the morning forgot his number, was one number off from the man next to him, and Walker stared us over with a shake of his head. As our numbers matched what they should be, Walker, in the direct center of the column, stood rigid. "Platoon, Atten-hut! Right Face!" Each word was broken with a pause, and the o's in "platoon" were always drawn-out, turning our frayed nerves into an evergreen bough with too much snow. Any moment the heavy snow would drop and the energy release. The release. The column moved as one in practiced foot movements that thundered off the concrete walls around us. "Forward March!"

His tenor began singing the steps in a tune that rose and fell to the percussion of our rubber soles. I never failed to be motivated by the snap-lock precision of a well-drilled platoon. Our faces continued to reach deeper shades of red as the hours in the hot San Diego sun whittled away. We practiced for the initial drill assessment a week later, over and again, we thundered up and down the asphalt square, repeating movements until all hundred of us moved as a single entity. Drill was beauty, drill was discipline. Drill was always fucked up by someone out of step. Every time a footfall was out of place, we did it again. And again.

It is the unswerving and unthinking instant obedience to orders that is the hallmark of the Marines. I really do not believe that the quality of people who join differing branches of the military is any or much different. Men and women who are brave and selfless will be such in any branch and with any amount of training. The discipline the Marines provides supplements for those of us who are not awarded with much in the nature of fearlessness. And all of this starts in the crucible of Boot Camp.

1. There was Smithy, a chubby guy with little scared eyes and a head that was really too small for his body. He tried hard, no matter the unwanted attention given to him. He often wet the bed, and I knew from day one that I wanted him as my sparring partner when we learned to fight. If boot camp taught me anything, it was to identify weaker men and capitalize on the opportunity.
2. Gomez was one of those short kids from Chicago who simply exuded toughness. Gomez basically sweat hardness and a pitiless drive. And when one day, after the platoon was beaten into the dirt because of me, he threatened to kill me in the showers that night, I shook knowing he meant it.
3. Zardin grew up in San Bernadino County, and somehow always managed to work that into conversation. "This recruit is from Temecula, sir," was an excited cry from the back of the formation, presumably in response to the question of where anyone else was from. He was average and grew up in a Marine Corps family. His father retired as a Gunnery Sergeant. One day when the drill instructors found this out, they called him, and Zardin's dad told the instructors to beat him raw. They did not even wait to hang up the phone. I like to imagine Zardin Sr. laughing as he heard the yells and cries on the other end.

Everything continued to revolve around discipline and the formation of a core in each person that was tough and unbreakable. The idea was that each of us would break.

My moment of breaking occurred on an early morning seven- or eight-weeks in. We moved from MCRD to Camp Pendleton for field exercises and rifle training, and I felt so surprised and fortunate that my time had not yet come. The drill instructors had the habit of not allowing any recruit to have more than twenty or thirty seconds for our morning piss.

Every person knew that when you wake up in the morning, you will die if you do not piss. This was an especially poignant fact for the Marine recruit. We drank anywhere from one to three liters of water before bed on line, forced hydration. I trained myself to wake up in the middle of the night to piss. When morning comes, we lined up to share a toilet with six or seven others in a frantic communal pee, running away the second before totally finished, so the bouncing and pleading recruit behind you won't explode. This morning in the second phase, there was no piss break, and in a fatal miscalculation, I did not wake up early. I was a ticking time bomb.

We marched down to breakfast, and I could almost feel the squishing in my boots of what was about to be an ammonia foot bath. I maintained my bladder control with minimal grimaces and only small whines. My only hope was to eat breakfast faster than anyone else and run outside to where we formed up to march on and begin the day. My half-baked plan was to act like a squad leader (who had special privileges) and make my way behind the building and find some wall for a quick release. Why not the cafeteria, you ask? Well, the only bathrooms I knew of were Marine only, and I didn't really want to meet my drill instructor in the next stall over. Exploding from distended bladder would then have been the least of my problems.

It all started well. No one had followed me, and I found a wall at the back of the cafeteria that was waiting to become a urinal. With an audible groan, I began to help myself out until from behind me, a shadow grew. Neither of us spoke as I turned my head in what seems to be slow motion and locked eyes with my doom. A huge man-shaped shadow with a drill instructor's campaign cover was looming over me like the pillar of fire loomed over the Egyptians when they were chasing the Israelites in Egypt. My life was now fully over.

I was smoked (given extra physical punishment usually for up to fifteen minutes of intense activity while yelling a response to the instructor a time) up to seven or eight times that day. The whole platoon's training schedule was put on hold so I could be made an example of. That night, I had death threats whispered in my ear. Fellow recruits, many of whom I counted as friends the morning before, were threatening dismemberment. Gomez glared at me from across the squad bay, and I could not, could not summon the courage to meet his eyes.

Many of these guys were escaping the LA, Chicago, and New York gangs, and there was nothing a little farm kid who couldn't grow facial hair and who yelled like a little girl sucking helium could do to stop it. I earned the label of the platoon bitch for all of second phase, and all but a few helped to make each moment miserable. I had my allies. I had friends who stood up to others for me, and I am sure I owe them my life. I am sure they remember who they are, and I thank them sincerely.

Three months passed by in a blur of training, suffering, and self-loathing, during which I wanted to beat my own ass for making the decision to become a Marine.

Despite the best efforts of my drill instructors, I graduated. I remember that one of them, Sgt. Michelson, remarked to me during the graduation ceremonies as he handed me my coveted Eagle Globe and Anchor, the hallmark and symbol of the Marine, "You only half deserve this, you little piece of shit." His hand hesitated over mine, and his eyes were cold and detached. I thought for a few moments, I might be denied in front of my family. However, his hand placed the symbol in my sweaty and trembling palm.

"Yes sir, thank you, sir," I stammered in a soft voice, staring at a spot in between his eyes. I tried not to cry, not in shame of his hatred, but through all the pain and frustration of the past few months, this seemingly unattainable piece of black metal meant more to me than any other thing I ever achieved before. Even half earning it, I earned it. I fulfilled my greatest ambition in life. I could now always be a Marine. But why did I only half deserve it? I screwed up a few times, no more really than anyone else. I did well on all my exams and fitness, my marksmanship and field tests, maybe he just did not like me. We don't have to like everyone, but the bold as brass way he said it was astonishing. Apparently, that day when my parents came and met him, he gave them compliments about me and said I would make a "fine Marine." We do strange things in the moment.

With that inauspicious beginning, I flew home for ten days of sleeping in until zero seven-hundred, and regardless of trying to break the habit, I still was taking five-second shits, to the amazement of the rest of my family.

I remember shaking hands with all of my drill instructors, even Sgt. Michelson. Most of all, I wanted to see my senior drill instructor, who I would have given anything to follow into combat.

I remember his smiling round face, his ears that stuck way too far out of his head, his face scarred from years in the infantry, and his deep love for rugby. He looked me in the eyes as I shook his hand and told me I would make a fantastic Marine. He said the same to my parents standing behind me. Then the pride came, the tears, the gratification, built and worry sank down.

I remember one night before graduation, my senior drill instructor wanted all hundred of us to sing the Marine Corps Hymn before bed. The hymn was something sacred, and rarely were we found worthy of an acapella rendition. The song spoke to us of battles fought and heroes created. In the Marines, heroes were not created by killing lots of people; rarely were we taught about those men. No, heroes were those who gave their lives for their friends and the strangers they were sent to protect. It was the people who jumped on grenades, stormed machine gun emplacements, withstood capture and torture, and reshaped our world through their sacrifice.

We sang deep and loud. The sound waves bounced off the walls and drifted off into other squad bays where frightened and unworthy recruits stood at attention and listened to the choir. Staff Sgt. Walker stood directly in front of me at attention and looked through me at the faces of men he once served with as I sang the hymn and shook as the words pumped through my veins, transmogrifying from language to emotion. A single tear dripped down his cheek as we stood there.

When all verses were finished, he looked around at all of us and walked proudly back into his duty hut.

Within seven months of my graduation, Staff Sgt. Walker and most of his squad drove into an ambush and would be dead, shot through a dozen times on the streets of Ramadi while attempting to cover the withdrawal of his men.

It was so easy to strut in uniform. Following my ticket to Los Angeles, I changed out of my civilian clothes into my Service Alpha uniform in the bathroom outside the USO. I was off to the School of Infantry. This school was what would change me from Marine to infantry Marine, the exclusive club of men—and now women, thank god—who are experts in attack and ambush and fear and silence.

The Alphas were my favorite uniform. They were an olive-green form-fitting but somewhat rough gabardine fabric that would make even the skinniest weakling look like a muscle-bound trained monster. Even me. The Alphas were a business suit, a new skin, a fragment of the new identity we would cling to all our lives. The tan shirt and tie underneath reminded me of the service uniform World War II soldiers wore while on leave. In fact, it has not changed much from that very one from seven decades before. The dress uniform, with its high collar, adorned enlistment posters from World War I and before. It was all steeped in history and lore and that is what gave it power over us. We were, not felt like, but actually were a recreation of those faces from the past.

I waited for a white unmarked bus to take me and most of my graduating class from the airport to Camp Pendleton, the main west coast base an hour south of LA.

In infantry school, with companies of two to three hundred Marines, we spent hours each day learning the intimacies of infantry tactics. We marched everywhere. We fired the M249 Squad Automatic Weapon, we learned how to shoot AT-4 rocket launchers, we learned patrolling tactics, and we learned how to march. We learned how to keep silent and move swiftly in gear, avoiding detection, and all about small unit warfare. Most of all we became masters of marching. We came to call it "humping." These were just surface lessons. The real lessons would be instilled by our squad and team leaders months later when we graduated this step and went to our real operating units.

After this month, we were able to pick our desired specialty within the infantry discipline. Well, we were allowed to at least make a wish list. The instructors reflected on the past month's performance as well as our mental ASVAB scores to determine who would be best suited for what job. The regular foot infantry (0311) would inevitably be those whose physical fitness and accuracy with the M-16 were their strengths. The same would be for machine gunners (0331), but they preferred an individual style of thinking out of the box as well as the ability to hump an incredible amount of gear. Mortar men (0341) preferred math skills. I wanted to be an Assault man (0351). Assault men became part engineer, part anti-tank, and part tactician. We had to be skilled in creative and quick thinking. Our job was to overcome seemingly insurmountable problems and barriers on the battlefield with quick and level-headed solutions involving lots of C-4 or TNT.

Once chosen, I merged with my new little clique of future assault men and spent the remaining two months of school exclusively studying my new field. Regular infantrymen would spend most nights in the field, training on small-unit patrolling and weapons proficiency. The assault men spent most days and nights in the classroom staring at calculations of how much C-4 it would take to destroy a bridge, build a tank trap, or how to identify a Russian T-72 tank from its similar brother the T-62, and how to construct expedient explosives such as Bangalore torpedoes and claymore mines from scratch and a little C-4. I won't say I excelled, but I did well, passing all my tests the first time around, which was more than I could say for some.

Where boot camp was all about mental training, this period geared towards moving forward as a trained operator and Marine. Drill and much of the mental torture went by the wayside. We focused instead on physical training—muscle memory drills with our weapon systems and heavy hikes.

This is not to say the games and torture were over. The training schedule built long hikes starting from a five-kilometer up to a twenty-five-kilometer march all in full gear. Often before the marches, an instructor would order several men to empty their packs and confirm the whole packing list had been met. Regardless of the length, we stuffed a sleeping system, change of clothes, three liters of water in canteens, various containers and bags, a gas mask system, food, socks, survival gear, and many other items in the backpack. On the body, we wore our flak jacket, helmet, rifle, and more water. For the specialty platoon, we also divided up several machine guns, mortar systems, anti-tank rocket systems, and inert ammunition.

On the last march up and down the scrub ridges of Camp Pendleton, weapons platoon men proved our grit. We started near the back of the formation, which included all of Bravo Company, roughly two-hundred men. We marched within arm's length of each other. The goal was to help push the man in front if he starts to fall back. The route started up a long steep hill of around five hundred meters. We all did well. The next hill started to make men slow. By the third hill, we struggled. The old jeep trails, deeply rutted and soft, make for poor footing. I started out without any piece of a weapon system, and by the beginning of this hill, snatched the fifty-pound .50 caliber M-2 receiver off a struggling machine gunner. No one offered any verbal support to push us. Our heads were down, and one foot in front of the other moved us slowly up the hill. I caught glimpses of regular grunts falling out around our formation, and we heckled them, spitting disdain and insults. Platoons are supposed to support their men and make sure no one falls out. A big machine gunner even grabbed a full pack off a struggling Marine to give him a few minutes respite. Halfway up the hill, the same man, sporting two packs and two rifles, kept in formation, forcing the hurting man to hold onto the loops on the back of his pack. He was pulling the man up the hill.

At the top, we paused for fifteen minutes and recovered. Our boots came off, and we massaged blistering flesh. The struggling recovered their gear and softly listened to advice from instructors. At the end of the time, all stood and donned gear and weapon systems. I traded my receiver for a mortar tripod. A mile into the next section, hill four loomed over us, yet another obstacle. The weak were forced to the front; we resolved to use sheer force of weight to push them over the hurdle.

One of my instructors was a terrifying man. His muscles bulged out of his cammies, and his eyes flared at any weakness. His voice boomed like an artillery barrage when he became angry. Midway up the hill, his laughter reached me as I gagged, and snot began to run down my face. My eyes burned, and each desperate breath became fire. He thought it was a good joke to pop a tear gas grenade at the head of our platoon and make us walk through it without gas masks. We grabbed the man in front of us, and the blind led the blind through the cloud of particulates that the wind blew up the hill with us. He stood at the summit just laughing.

As an assault man, I spent long hours in the dimly lit classroom with a few of us who were chosen. Instead of drill instructors who yelled at us incessantly and beat us down, we engaged in a teacher-student relationship with our new instructors. They were with us from morning until evening and created an air of competence and respect. I liked my instructors and most of the students.

Two guys from Chicago deemed themselves the toughest and wanted to fight anyone who they thought was 'mouthy.' They deemed me undesirable, and I was challenged to fight often. Always, I found a way out, but mainly I was afraid. The main Chicago tough guy was a real fighter, and there was no way my small frame would withstand the pummeling he planned to give me. Even though my record of fighting and winning is low, I was getting better at accumulating friends and allies who stood by me. In this way, I was able to squirm my way out of any fight.

There are many good ways of fighting. One, like these self-proclaimed tough guys (and the preferred method of Marines in infantry school), was to jump into the fray and pound away until superior power was attained, or the other person was beaten down. There was no shame in that, they said. The second method was mine. I made friends. I made compatriots, usually fellow small guys, who could gang up to achieve superior firepower. This is really the doctrine of the Marines. Fire superiority in small and large units. The man who stands alone really is nothing. The man who stands with others committed has the real upper hand. At least, that's how I justify suspected cowardice. At the heart of the matter was a desire to not have tears beat out of me.

The instructors often tried to teach us that this new war we were fighting would involve us to the largest degree. They had those of us who were planning on going infantry raise our hands one day. About a quarter were intending to do infantry or combat arms (tanks, artillery, amphibious vehicles, etc.). The rest were moving into support jobs that had little to do with potential combat, but the Marines forced everyone to think like an infantryman while in boot camp. Once, before we split into our specific specialties, we marched into a room with a screen. Our instructors were standing up in front of the stage and began talking openly about what we would encounter soon after graduation. The pictures of dead bodies and combat that had been recorded in Afghanistan and the invasion of Iraq flashed one after another. We looked around at each other. I was not expecting this.

Congealed blood matted against the hair of one man whose head exploded. Crying children knelt beside crumpled and lifeless forms. I was transfixed. The scene flashed. Marines patrolled down the alleys. The video shook, and soft Arabic voices whispered prayers to Allah. The deep rumble of a Russian machinegun burst the forced silence. The Marines dropped to the ground and began engaging the hidden enemy. The farther off high pop of American fire whipped and cracked past the camera. The music lifted in a glorious salute to the men who did their duty and killed Americans. The tune swelled and dropped. The video cut out before the Marines had the chance to counter-attack. The last scene illuminated clearly two bodies that did not move. They wore armor, and helmets and the blood coagulated and matted in their hair and on their clothing. The flies became legion before the body emptied of blood. They alighted on eyeballs, lips, wounds, any surface. Later, I knew, Marines would kneel beside the forms, heads bowed, shoulders dropped. Their hands swatted at the flies in a hopeless attempt to keep the body sacred. The tears would mingle with the blood, and the cycle would continue.

DECEMBER 2011
Moscow, Idaho

What do I find terrifying—like utterly chilling, the kind of scared where logic and reason leave replaced with simply a visceral response?

Being alone.

What makes me sweat is bolting awake in the dark, convinced you have seen something or someone in the shadows. It's having a dream where your long-dead friends gather around the bed and talk coherently, have a conversation, discussing nothing in particular, and especially not anything of actual import, the only way one would expect a dead person to talk. Scary is realizing your dream is repeating itself in your head through the waking hours, some kind of replicating omen, a skipping record on a rotational speed set way too fast.

It's having the PRC-119 squad radio still strapped on your back day in and day out, the weight becoming part of you, the crackle of the half fowled earpiece—one of the beauties of the heat of the desert—in your ears years after you last clipped one of those black plastic phone handles of the radio to your helmet strap and wedged it onto your ear, so you didn't need to lift the headset from loops on your body armor—a minor inconvenience, but one none the less—the headset automatically slipping in your ear sweat and fouling. The radio crackling even when you are back home on the couch with your spouse or drinking with friends at a bar, the casualty report spelled out slow and deliberate, no mistakes.

Gunfighter, this is Gunfighter four the voice came through the headset every day for years, and each word hit like the thwack crossbow bolt into the target. *We hit a VBIED. Break. We have taken several casualties. Break. We are RTB for CASEVAC, over.* The voice is one of muffled terror. The voice on the other end, all too well known, is wavering and cracks. Is he in pain? Perhaps he is wounded too. Perhaps they are in a firefight. Go outside, listen. No. Nothing besides the reverberation of explosions and potshots that are constantly playing out across the city.

Silence.

The silence dropped me on my knees in the middle of a hot day, when people should be hunkering down in the shade. The only patrol out, mine, the one I opted not to go on. The one where I was seated, ready to leave for a routine mission. I could imagine what was happening. The truck swerving across the median from the unbroken straight line of our convoy, the green armor bristling with swaying gun barrels while downtown Fallujah all came out to see which of the American group was hurt this time. Or perhaps the vehicle was too disabled to move, and the dust was being kicked up by Marines rushing around in the mess of downtown hooking up a tow bar while security punched out, everyone ready to kill, guns off safety, fingers on the trigger, someone about to do something stupid and justified to someone innocent.

The silence following the moment after the blast a mile away rocketing the truck sideways, peppering everything with red hot iron, hidden blood spraying from the heads and shoulders above the armor the moment after a man driving a white van too close to the patrol closed his eyes and connected wires completing the circuit setting off two 155-millimeter artillery rounds. Over one hundred pounds of explosives vaporized in less than an instant.

The acronyms are still fresh in my mind and come back after more than a decade since hearing them. The voice is forcibly calm, but still containing the slightest hint of panic creeping in. They were on a routine pickup mission before grabbing the rest of us and heading down to the entry control point into Fallujah. But that is the way all these dreams begin for me. The radio squawking hoarsely like a chronic smoker. The voice returns the casualty call almost immediately in the dream.

This is Gunfighter, we are standing by to evacuate the wounded when you return. Break. Standing by for nine-line. Over.

Uh, first casualty Echo Seven, Delta, Oscar, Bravo, Bravo, India, November, Sierra. Translating in my mind Echo Seven: Gunnery Sergeant, D-O-B-B-I-N-S, our platoon sergeant. Someone botched the report, badly, but the phonetic names hit me, each letter a blow knocking me lower and lower until I was buffeted by a sneaker wave, a storm surge of letters and names taking my feet out from under me and dragging me out to depths. These were men who I ate with, cried with, slept next to, patrolled with for years. In my dream and in real life, the sweat and panic come not at the blast—those were common enough—but at the names read.

***

The year was 2012. It had been a half dozen years since I separated. I still felt it though. I was at home in Idaho next to my wife in a dark room on a soft bed, drenched in sweat. I wandered back five years after my first deployment in 2004, Al Anbar province, into the murk of attempted repression and back deeper. I rolled over, facing the wall and the side table that held a pistol in a small safe, one magazine inserted into the handle, two others snugged next to the gun. There were twenty-one rounds in total. I rolled back over slow and softly to not wake my wife who is a light sleeper. I just had the dream again, and I knew it would be a long time before going back to sleep.

I sat up on the flannel sheets and quietly walked out of the bedroom, closing the open door behind me carefully, turning the handle and putting my finger in the frame before closing it fully. I poured a drink of good single malt scotch, two fingers high, and added a little water with clammy and shaky fingers. The first sip washed out the bitter acid, the next few helped wash over the memories, giving them a translucent film. I just stood at the counter of our small house, and eventually sat down on a stool. The Douglas fir stools glowed softly from the reflection of street light off a new blanket of snow and the little ice crystals floating down to cover up the dead of the fall.

There needed to be a change. I knew it my wife, Abbie, knew it, my parents knew it. I was drinking more than usual, I was moody. I sunk into melancholy and depression without effort. At my second pour of scotch, I had talked myself into calling the VA again and trying to find a counselor. I had one before, years before in Portland, and loved how she helped me learn to deal with the rage and irrationality that popped up constantly in my head, leaking into my heart and my everyday life. I sat on the stool and just watched the snow fall like glass shards till my head drooped, and I walked back to bed to lie awake.

THERAPY
January 2012
Spokane, Washington

The waiting room of my local Veterans Affairs hospital is a cesspit of frustration, depression, and the lingering stench of medicine breath. The people working the counters are certainly well-meaning enough, but the cat calendar hanging behind the desk and encouraging me to "chill out" does nothing to alleviate the deeply rooted feelings that have seeped into the whole of the building. No matter how hard the regular employees and doctors within the VA work to repair their image, sadly, the VA health care system will always be tarnished and full of stereotypes. No matter how many visits I have that are positive, I will always wonder when the next negative one will be.

My semi-local hospital is in Spokane, Washington, a two-hour drive from home. The interior is stuffed with cheap furniture and threadbare carpet that cause more medical problems than the occupants have before getting in; the carpet seems decades old and worn down to nubbins and covered in shoe leavings, more hardwood than carpet. In one corner by the main door, in a busy coffee shop where one can also buy a variety of military unit patches in case someone came in without theirs, there is a hand-painted thermometer with the mercury less than a third full toward some fundraising goal. In the first year, I went to Spokane, it didn't change once, the second and third years it also remained the same, the streaks of red mercury fading slightly slower than the fundraiser. The VA always seems to be fundraising for one thing or another. I find it hard to imagine that with all the excess and waste in the military budget, the VA hospital administration needs to fundraise for a new dialysis machine, or espresso maker, or CT scan machine.

***

My footsteps echoed down the heart of the building at right angles through a labyrinth of geometrical hallways with green road sign tacked to the walls labeled "Patriot Lane" and "Hero Way" and other equally absurd parotitic claptrap that are supposed to make me feel loved and respected but sustain only an acute discomfort and feeling of silliness.

See, I've never really wanted to be the kind to boast about my patriotism and live in a world of red-white-and-blue tchotchkes. No disrespect if that is you, but it makes me vaguely uncomfortable.

I feel no connection to the anthem or flag. They are great unifiers and necessary to any nation, but I rarely ever get goosebumps when hearing the anthem, or seeing the flag bounce down the roads during parades. Don't think I don't love where I live. Or that I don't love the people that live here. I just have seen too much insanity erupt from the mission that sense of veiled nationalism gives us. There was a big part of my life where I loved all that stuff. I wore my camouflage pants, cut into shorts with the nametags still sewn on to show others my affiliation. I worked my years in the military into conversations that were not related to it at all. See, I wanted to be part of the Marines again, I wanted to feel like someone again, I wanted to have a purpose, even if it were to participate in those mindless wars we've been so accustomed to. I feel that the Marines in particular imbue us with an understanding that we are always bound to the oath to country we made years ago. While that tribalism gives us a community of purpose, when that is shunted off, we are easily lost.

I only come to the hospital for the gently named "behavioral health ward." I came for therapy and an hour of time that helped more than any self-medication ever had before—regardless of the quality of scotch.

The behavior health ward in Spokane was a brand-new building annex connected to the main hospital, though the carpet was still nubbins and the furniture still torture. The new building was nice with exposed wood on metal and beautiful angular lines bringing the eye to the floor-to-ceiling windows reflecting a little gravel garden where several employees sat on a snow-covered chair and smoked while trying to huddle together away from the blowing snow. I have always thought being a smoker in the northwest during winter is an exercise in masochism. After sitting on a chair that gave my back a faint ache, I jumped at a soft and kind voice.

"Hello, you must be Mr. Warmbier." I smiled as the plump and kindly face reached me. Over the phone, when making my appointment, I requested a "motherly woman" as a therapist, and for once, the VA got things right. Everyone seeking mental health care wants something different. I have found that a grandmotherly or motherly type of woman has helped me more than a man of any age.

I looked up at her and half smiled, "I am Paul, it's nice to meet you." I stammered and stood a little too fast, aware of betraying some nervousness.

"I'm Marla," she said plainly as she walked ahead of me, turning around once or twice to smile and make sure I was still with her. Sitting in the waiting room prior to all this would only be less fun if I woke up to find out someone removed all my bones while I slept. A person can only read the Salvation Army's monthly magazine so much before willing death. Thank god for smartphones.

She let me into her room and followed me in, flipping a little cue card sign on her door, signifying there was a session in progress. The room was small, though I imagined with just the two of us in there, there was plenty of room. In fact, I figured we felt too close together by the time the whole thing was done. Therapy tends to shrink the room and force intimacy. I really didn't choose to start these sessions, nor did I choose to file a claim for PTSD. My wife, family, and nightmares helped me choose.

I don't want to sound ungrateful; I knew it was the next stage. My family has been dropping hints for years; my wife was very nice about it. "You know you have insurance through the VA. Just head up there today. We have nothing planned," she would say over breakfast. Bless her. There were hints mornings after particularly bad dreams, hints after drinking much more than I should have, or after I spent time drinking alone, and there were hints after angry outbursts at inanimate objects and random people. I just thought I had a short temper, but it turned out, just about everything set me into a rage in those days.

I filed for disability through the VA, citing my two tours to Iraq, and almost immediately—well within two months, but remember VA time operates on its own rules and disregards the standard laws of time and space—I felt the vibration of my phone. I asked for a counselor sooner rather than later, and this is where it all began.

"Well, Mr. Warmbier, how are you?" Marla said as she sat down in front of me. She sounded chipper. Too friendly, I have always been wary of people who are overly friendly. I always wonder what their angle is. I guess it never really strikes me that they may not have an angle at all, but are simply trying to be nice and sincere. I smiled that kind of pained half no-tooth smile in return to her greeting. My stomach ached something awful, it was that weird mix of hunger and nerves that made me think I was going to puke everywhere. Best to keep my mouth shut until it subsided. "Well, Mr. Warmbier, or can I call you Paul?" she waited, and I nodded. "Paul, I read over your file from your previous visits in Portland, Oregon, and I am interested in what you would like to achieve from these meetings." The wave passed, and I felt in control again. *Deep breath*. I concentrated, in then out. It was amazing how much concentration those usually automatic movements took.

I met her dark brown, almost jet-black eyes. Took in her medium-heavy build, the kind of build that made me appreciate her. She was a real person. Pictures of several kids sat on her desk. She carried the reminder of the children, and despite how she felt about that, I appreciated it. I like people who have *blemishes*. I think it's evidence of reality and permission to be normal. She was muscular, thick-set, real, not one of those fitness freaks. I have never really been able to trust them either. Someone who denies food and alcohol for "health" isn't someone I see eye-to-eye with.

"Well..." I paused. One word out, that was the hard part, it always has been. It's always easier to keep talking once the first word choked itself out. "In the past, I spent a lot of time thinking about anger and nightmares and self-esteem." She nodded, and though I paused, I let one more phrase drip down like tears, and it terrified and shamed me, "Oh, and I worry about suicide."

It didn't seem like she wanted to interrupt and ask one of those annoying shrink questions like: *Would you tell me more about your anger?* "At my previous sessions in Portland, we tried to find where the worries came from, but shortly before I left Portland, we started to talk about triggers. My old therapist mentioned something called CBT but we ran out of time to try." She smiled and again didn't interrupt. I smiled back for real for the first time. (Cognitive behavioral therapy—if I may simplify the term, I would say it's a way to get to the core issues and redirect negative and unhelpful thought processes that lead to actions and mentalities.) When she seemed to think I was not going to continue, she nodded sagely. Too sagely perhaps, she only looked around forty, and I am not sure sage nods should be allowed until one reaches at least sixty, but that may be colored by jealousy because I don't remember a time I rated sage nods.

"And I worry about suicide because it seems to come and go in almost overwhelming urges. The urges are there and then either I want to act on them or they get better for a time. I have lost too many friends to suicide so far," I grabbed a tissue from the box next to me with a fast motion as I choked the last two sentences out. "I don't want to act on the urge when I am down. It scares me." I blinked a lot, and a feeling of shame and then anger at the shame took over everything. My head dropped, "I'm afraid of myself."

No reaction. "Well, Paul, I appreciate you sharing this with me; the start of these things can often be hard. However, since you have an idea of what you would like to cover, or deal with, a good amount of the process has begun for us already. Concerning dreams, have you ever taken medicine for your sleep?"

I bridled. "No," I said flatly. "I am definitely not interested in becoming a sedated vegetable."

She smiled and tapped her fingers on her leg. "Ok." And she switched tack immediately. "Sometime, I would love to talk to you about triggers, just like your previous therapist started to but we can get to that when you are ready." She began to introduce triggers in a soft and empathetic voice. I had rarely heard the term, but all of my previous sessions in Portland began to be more coherent. In many veterans, especially those who think they can tough it out, triggers, until identified, are terrifying mysteries. Things to be avoided. A trigger is something that sets into motion a physical or emotional response relating to experiences or trauma. Triggers, however, may not always be related to the specific trauma. She insists this past point with utmost sincerity and I listen hard. For everyone, they are different. A person may react to a situation enough times to recognize that they should avoid that particular scenario or action, but it is not that easy when we discuss triggers that revolve around more than the things we can touch and manipulate.

"I think there are things that I see most in vets who come in here as a different kind of triggers." She paused to count them off on her fingers. I nodded effusively. She tells me that triggers can be anything from sights, smells, the way the wind blows on your face at night like it used to on a late-night ambush, it can be how people talk to you, it can be a car backfiring, it can also be *nothing* happening. She paused and extends her hand, allowing me to take over control again.

I think for a while, trying not to meet her eye, and not really realizing it, I was becoming much less irritable in the conversation. "The three main triggers," I begin slowly, looking at my hands wringing a bugger-filled tissue, "seem to revolve around smells or sounds like what I knew in Iraq, physical actions or interactions, and certain dates and times. They come and remind me and almost send me into a spiral I don't often see coming."

"Indeed. Paul, I am interested in what makes you positive. I am not talking about the simple 'what inspires you' kind of talk, but the real discussion of what drives you and what drives your triggers. In our sessions, I would really like to explore what your purpose is. Often I see that purpose is lost for veterans, particularly combat veterans." Marla paused and let me sink into the philosophical stupor I tend to get into when contemplating. Maybe she knew more about me than I knew. I loved philosophy, almost made it a major in college but stuck with something I could get a job with.

"Please continue. I'd love to hear about you." I sat, slightly agog – what was it that really drove me? And in a way, what was it that drove me to join the Marines, choose infantry, interact with people in the way I did? I don't think it would suffice to simply answer with the usual "well, I wasn't going to college," which was true nonetheless.

I joined in a time of war and knew from the first invasion—I was in high school—to the time my boots fell on the asphalt and wavy heat of Kuwait what I was going to do. What I didn't prepare for was how it would all change me, how it would mold me into something with multiple faces.

I mentioned suicide to her in the beginning, half intentionally, half hoping she wasn't really paying attention. I never liked mentioning the topic but the worry of *it* had been sticking me deep then. These days, I mention it more easily because I have accepted it as a commonality among many people. Many people I've known have known someone who has tried to or succeeded in committing suicide, or has attempted it themselves. We don't talk about it, but need to.

Most people don't like recognizing what they fear most. I knew Marla took note of the word, but in calling no attention to it, I wondered if she took it seriously or didn't want to make it take over everything we discussed. Over the years, there have been many friends who either committed suicide or died in tragic accidents that I wondered suspiciously about. It was a terrifying ghost in the night. Suicide came and went, leaving no one behind and striking with such force and random effect I never knew who would be next. It could easily have been me. I often hear about the war we take home with us, but only recently did I really understand what that was. We bring war back, and it hangs over us for the rest of our lives.

These initial meetings always went so fast. We talked a lot about surface issues, we got to know one another, see if it would be a good fit. It was a date with high stakes. As our time wound down and we talked about identifying triggers, she gave me homework. "You are a teacher?" she asked as she stood and began walking to the door. I was a teacher; I was subbing and teaching in the middle school I was a student teacher for the previous year. "Your job before next week is to write your stories. I want you to write down as many of them as you can. Our stories define us, they make us, and if we remake them, they can be for good or ill." She nodded to herself. More writing. I smiled at this. This was something I could do. I wrote for fun, I had since I was a kid writing awful poetry about mountains and streams. If this was to be a therapy of stories, I would make sure I made the best use of it.

GUILT, 2019

It starts in my chest and surges outward like a wave. I imagine the wave is different for each sufferer, but for me, it begins deep in my chest, where my lungs take over my body and shove my heart to the side. The burning is tangible as I recount an experience that causes emotion. Slowly, the fear and shame crawl up me and out of me into the stomach and the head.

I thought that I would become desensitized to the feeling like I have for so many other emotions and events, but there is something about guilt, and its partner emotion that I cannot remove by self-hatred. The images rise up uncontrollably when I am playing with my children, talking with my wife, on a run, a hike, fly-fishing some stream. Sometimes I think my brain is laughing at me and waiting until I feel calm and free to bring them up. At times it's an interaction from that day. Others, it is what I helped do to that guy fifteen years ago.

Lately, it has been that last one. Since beginning writing this, I started a new course of therapy and have been talking to a non-VA therapist, a former Army medic who seems to be able to dredge up his own past when I am talking about mine. He always stares at me when I talk in a way that makes me think he is horrified by my words. I wonder if he was in during a time of war, or if he was in that period in the nineties. He rarely talks, lets my propensity for verbal connection guide my internal conversation, and I love it. I talk, ramble actually, and he writes notes on a large yellowed pad. He wears a fedora with a feather in it and a trench coat pulled tight around his waist like a hard-boiled detective. I think he is stuck in the wrong generation. He is a psychoanalyst, though I don't think it's Freudian.

I recently shared a memory with him that I had only ever hinted at with my best friend and former Corpsman, Ryan Mills. Mills is one of those people whose life seems to be predicated on those he saves. It is his existential purpose, and his reaction to the freedom we are all given. His responsibility. He is a monster of a man, nearly seven feet tall with flaming red hair. When I hug him, my head is buried in his shoulder like a child. He has a soft voice and deeply worried eyes. Those eyes have taken care of me for years. All of us seemed desperate to forget that day. For weeks and months after, we nearly baked the man who attacked our lieutenant, we laughed at our own cruelty, at our own willing brutality calling it "necessary" and "deserved."

These days, so many years later, I let it out for the first time after not mentioning it for over a decade. There is something in mentioning and simple innuendo that is so powerful. Even as I write these lines, I feel the tightness in my chest and gut, the twisting of my intestines into knots that threaten to make me disrupt the session and have to go shit myself out of anger and guilt again. But, because I have told this story recently, first to my new therapist as he sat with his notepad, paralyzed watching me sob into my hands as I told of the man who we detained after attacking us, listening as I relived once again what happened, again laughing as I watched and helped my squad, my brothers, my trusted ones do this. Dragging his wheezing frame into a cargo container, our makeshift detention facility, until Mills and our other corpsmen arrived and pushed their way through us and helped the man. Only they doing what humanity demanded. A fellow man, a human deserving of every aid. I remembered we shook our heads and told Doc to let him suffer.

Yes, we found bombs at his house. Yes, he punched our lieutenant. Yes, he could have been the one responsible for a few nights before when one of my closest friends, Rosie from third platoon, led a patrol into a bomb and had both legs ripped to pieces, flayed like a fish at the market from thigh to ankle by a buried cylinder of iron. He could have even been the guy who supplied the bomb that turned ten men from Echo company into pink mist and injured dozens more during an ill-conceived reenlistment ceremony outside of their base.

Movies taught me that normal people recoil when they see dead bodies. We are supposed to get a glimpse of blood and gore and bound for the nearest bush to vomit behind, especially if it is the first time. I never did. Not once did I recoil until many years after my deployment when I saw a dead girl in a heap in the ruined aftermath of the city of Tacloban in the Philippines when I was helping run a mission for Team Rubicon providing immediate disaster aid and rescue. Only then, instead of sick, I was sad.

I don't think I was a monster for not recoiling or

getting sick; however, I was too well mentally trained by the Marines. We would often watch videos in boot camp and infantry school where men would be beheaded or shot, we shared pictures of killed people, flies congregating around jagged bullet holes, bodies puffed up from the desert heat. In a surprisingly short length of time, the mind began to see that as the normal course of life. Heaps of bodies in a truck, legs, and arms ripped from torsos became nothing but meat and material. The Marines knows how to prepare men for war. Sadly, now we see high school kids and younger sharing access to these same types of photos. What was once a taboo that could get you court-marshalled has ended up becoming everyday interactions with the internet for kids.

Once on my second deployment, a man had blown himself up late at night while attempting to lay a bomb on the roadside. We heard the explosion and scrambled a QRF team. When we got there, a squad from third platoon was already there from a patrol. We rolled in hearing sardonic comments from the other squad's Marines like "Sure, just roll over a crime scene" and "No problem, just driving over fingers and toes." In a heap was what used to be a man. His rib cage was split open, and he looked like a prop from a 1980's B horror film. But that was what he was to us. Squatting down, looking into his chest cavity which had just exploded like a microwaved hotdog, I wasn't sick by the sight or smell; I was exhilarated. I loved it. One terrorist down. One less asshole in our way. This was how we were taught to think, to act.

And now, sitting in my office early in the morning with my daughter crawling around at my feet, there is something that is rising in my throat. Fifteen years too late.

I was angry then. I thought myself righteously indignant. It was all justified, wasn't it? We had lost many. Many killed, many injured, so much of our childhood had been turned into blood and dust, destroyed with the first bombs and the first time we raised our rifles and sighted in on a person, even that act without pulling the trigger was an affront to all we had been taught about humanity, magnanimity, humility, and love.

In the days and months and years leading up to the telling in the therapist's office, I punished myself. I slowly became surly, more than usual. I have always been a grump, but in my desire to detach those experiences from mine, I bore them all my own, not trusting anyone to bear them with me, to understand why I was so surly and angry at the world. I could handle them, right? I was tough enough. For god's sake, I was a Marine. I was supposed to be tougher than anyone alive. Sometimes, when I was alone at home, I sat crying, sometimes drunk, sometimes sober and occasionally stared at the pistol in my hand, wondering if I emptied my body of blood and brains if the guilt and pain would fade away and leave me forever. I would just hold it and think about what it would be like if I were dead. Would I go to heaven or hell? So many times in the Marines I did things where we walked away and said those words.

"We're going to hell for this."

As if I knew that it was an affront to all my understanding of God and who I should be. Could faith in God be enough to keep me from eternal suffering? Did others who perpetrated worse acts throughout history go to heaven regardless of their actions? Could faith and justification via my Lutheran understanding of theology be enough for any kind of redemption in this world or the next? Sometimes I think these questions lingering were the only things that kept me from pulling that trigger.

I put the gun to my head once and laid back on the plush pillow with it sticking up out of my head like a flag of a Conquistador. Looking at my wife's spot on the bed, I cried as the images of that man, other men, and women, and children we subjugated, hurt, didn't care for, killed, detained, abused or beat in some form or another all blew through my mind on repeat. I remember getting a text and reactively putting the gun back in the bedside cabinet and answering it. It was Ryan Mills. I don't remember what he said, what he wanted, but I knew that he had just saved my life once more.

Over the years, I have learned to channel the guilt I feel for how we treated people into creative outlets. I write, build furniture in my small woodshop, fly-fish, collect and read books obsessively. I spent three years helping build Team Rubicon, a tremendously powerful disaster relief organization. For four years my best friends and I started and operated a winery in Oregon making Pinot Noir. As the winery grew and the time requirements stacked up, and my wife had another baby, I had to leave, but I still love wine with a passion. I love to deconstruct it, find flavors, identify soils and locales that make each glass unique. Wine is an ever-changing evolution in the bottle. It does not stop changing until it impresses itself on you in your mouth. It rarely gives up. It rarely quits.

I seem to have the need to make to offset the destruction I happily engaged in years prior. By no means, again, do I feel alone in this. I look around at the community of veterans from my time period of war and see creators everywhere. MFA programs and trade mastery programs are chock-full of veterans eager to make and create. The wine industry has many veteran winemakers. Not only does society tell us to create and save our lives in the process, my generation, the lazy good-for-nothing millennials, are obsessed with creation, not necessarily for capitalistic gain but for the need to live in the creation and let it keep us alive. I believe that the act of creation is far more natural than that of destruction, especially later on in life when children come into the equation. Now, when I do think of the children whose lives I destroyed, my son's cherubic face is superimposed on theirs. I see him crying, wounded, killed and lying limp in a heap from a bomb or grenade. This, for those who do not have it, is one of the faces of PTSD. The mind is not our friend, and to those who have a traumatic brain injury or PTSD in some form, the mind is actively trying to destroy them. Everyday activity is an act of survival, avoidance of triggers, a grasping of nebulous hope.

The feeling is insidious. It takes over everything and rewires my brain to think only one way. Any interaction I have is replayed in my mind to find a way to be changed. Every mistake is magnified. Every action has alternatives that I should have followed. This is part of the problem with guilt and the long-term shame that pervades my mind since the war. To be honest, I have always been a person who feels emotions and worry more than many others, but as I have gotten older, the feeling seems to result in stronger reactions.

I hear the clichés all the time: my family are teachers, I love kids, it's not for the money. Those are all true for me, too, but I wonder if it is really due to my desire for penance. I want to change the world in a positive way to make up for all the negative I was responsible for.

2009, PORTLAND OREGON

When I sit at home alone, I usually make the mistake of watching the end of some movie like *Braveheart* or *Gladiator*. Usually, just the end. This is a mistake for me not simply because I cry uncontrollably, but because usually my whole night, if not longer, is shot. What is so moving to me is not necessarily the ending of some bloody struggle where the hero dies brutally, yet still heroically, standing up for his morals, but something entirely different.

I remember.

I remember the IEDs, the ambushes, the bloody lumps of men huddled like seeping trash piles along the road. I remember the horrid bits of war, and I usually try hard to do a good job of not remembering them, yet frustratingly enough, I am drawn to these memories. It hurts to remember. It pains me to look on my wrist and rub the words etched into the black painted aluminum band. The words are a scar and rubbing them only brings them out stronger.

OIF 2003-2007
Too many KIA – Never forgotten
Semper Fi Brothers.

It pains me to rub the words continually because faces shoot up my fingertips like electricity. They jolt directly to my brain and make me remember. It turns out memory is a double bullet. Despite the good times, when something triggers the synapses that bring the images up like vomit, the bad taste stays in my mouth long after the memory has passed.

I hear PTSD as a conversation piece thrown around a lot these days. Politicians love saying it. They love to slam one fist into the other hand while discoursing on some empty or vague pledge into a microphone. "Veterans are heroes!" or, "These men and women should not have to suffer like they do!" or my favorite is the "New Greatest Generation."

Yeah, I agree, we should not have to suffer like we do, but many of us do. And that is that, regardless of blame.

I relaxed in a bar around the fall of 2010, surrounded by others who were chatting amiably some with old friends, dates, and strangers. It was spitting rain outside. The water draining off the roof was a single, almost unbroken wall. Normally, I would have been depressed when socked in by so much rain, but often Portland rain is just accepted as a matter of course. Portland is one of those cities where when you sit in a bar all alone, you make several new friends with surprising swiftness. After one night at the bar, you may just end up with a few new roommates, whether you were looking or not; that is just the kind of town it is.

"Hey, remember that time when that first platoon guy blew shrapnel into Whitney's arm?" Someone, either Mills, Slavens, or I would say. We laughed at the misfortune, but only briefly, for we three began to sink into the change that accompanies the stage of understanding we are feeling.

Slavens and I met on my second day in the platoon in 2004. He was from Tacoma, Washington and lived day-by-day, adopting a slight grunge attitude from neighboring Seattle. He always had headphones with Beastie Boys or Rage Against the Machine playing. At the time, he seemed morose, quick to judgment, and fiercely proud but usually quiet about it. We called him 'mousy pants' because of his small narrow features and thin frame. He was a workhorse who always stood to do whatever job stood in our path regardless of the difficulty.

He just pursed his lips, darkened his small brown eyes, and got the job done. On patrol he was a team machine gunner and carried at times over a hundred pounds of gear over miles of foot patrols. He was an expert shot with any weapon he touched and knew it. Where I tried to dodge jobs, he always did them without much grumbling. Slavens was a natural born leader. He led by example and, taking the lead from Armas, grew into the best leader I have known.

I envied Slavens for the quick respect people had for him. When, on the second deployment he became a squad leader, he stood up for a deep injustice within the platoon. He stood up for his men and lost his position as squad leader and was kicked out of the platoon by new platoon leadership. He gained undying respect from his men by leading them well and keeping them safe.

If you have seen one arm full of shrapnel caused by a well-meaning friend trying to help, you've seen them all. You've seen one desert that stretched for eternity broken only by rivers containing water so real the blue reminds you of something you have seen only in a dream, waters that were diamonds in the morning and well, you know; you've seen them all. Except for the water, I have yet to see anything like it since.

"Remember how the nights were so utterly black at first, then the stars would pop out..." the voice trailed off and all three of us, alone, silent, remembered. The pockmarked blood spots from Whitney's wound seared into my memory, replaced by a night sky immense, utterly encapsulating, and brightly lit with new stars and the cosmic trail of the milky way stretching unbroken from horizon to horizon. I would look around at the lighthearted kindly strangers at the bar and feel so separated from them. It was only three of us against the whole of my world. We would take quick and deep pulls from our beer, occasionally snorting the foam back into the glass when a new and particularly vivid memory resurfaced. Home was a bubble that surrounded the camaraderie of these guys. When we separated, we seemed to dissipate the sense and the bubble that kept us comfortable burst as easily as it was recreated. Home is a word without meaning for many of us. It is something that everyone expected us to embrace when we came back to America after deployments, but what they didn't, couldn't understand was that it was a word that had been blown to pieces.

Glossary of Stuck Points #1: Home is a place that no longer exists, and it would be easier to stop looking for.

There is always a concentration of tissue boxes in the therapist's office. They are always full, no matter which therapist I go to. It's as if I am the only user, but that is absurd.

It is a strange world one belongs to when they become a veteran. I'm not talking about folks who sat at computer desks on huge bases in Iraq or Afghanistan, never witnessing the struggle, but we who went weeks without showers and clean clothing due to operational tempo. I'm talking about the people who would get out and watch the stars where there was no light in the whole universe except for the eternal night's glimmering provided by the vast emptiness around us. Or those who would walk the Euphrates and Tigris in a hundred pounds of gear, running gloved hands through the tall grasses as the moonlight shimmered down like rain, like they used to do along stream beds back home until the low groan of incoming mortars crashed in and broke apart the stars and river and grasses into a million pieces of stardust. The blood, leaving pools in the dust, dripped down the grass, coating gloved fingers in a jelly. How does that person, how did I and these three other men, come home and survive the onslaught of chaos that is an ordinary life? In a way, I envy the others at the bar. In a way, I pity them.

Either way, I do not feel home and have no idea if I will

ever be able to find that place again beside the Euphrates where the birds warbled in high arias, and the occasional warm breeze wafted the weight of the sun in lazy waves where the kids came running up, smiles so wide and so honest you thought they would hurt. I'd like to say as we laughed and sighed that I felt at home with them.

A while back, I was reading Anthony Swafford's *Jarhead*. The opening pages begin by sorting gear, and I remember that same moment shortly after my discharge in 2007 taking a break from some college paper and going to the moldering pile of my own gear. Though mine differed from Swafford's and the Gulf War era gear, I still sifted through it, and much of mine, dribbled out sand from far away deserts. I laid out my desert cammies. There were a few small bloodstains from little things like snagging my arm on a rusty door hinge or a random piece of jagged rebar while assaulting an HVT's compound or helping a wounded Marine or civilian whose blood would co-mingle with my other coagulated stains, indistinguishable from one another. Terrorist, native, friendly, all blood dried into the same stain, regardless of how the American officials tried to convince us that we were superior beings.

On the blouse, I still have a line of crusted human salt. I washed the blouse after deployment almost a decade ago, but it still held firm, forming a new outline like chalk on the dark street after a shooting. They boasted rips and tears, and after two deployments were actively dissolving under the weight of misuse. The wind sandblasted them and the fabric was softer than puppy fur.

An old harness hung from my hands, coming clean from the plastic tub. The slightly green duty belt looped

through stood, still flecked with tan spray paint. It held
grenade pouches, magazine pouches and ammo drum
bags and was almost white from the sun. Some of these I
took off Gunny Dobbin's bloodied and torn flak vest in
2005 after the medevac stormed out of the base to Fallujah
Surgical. The bottom of one bag, I tried to re-sow
inexpertly with thick black thread, frayed on the ends from
some unremembered fragment passing by. The articles
shared stories where 'do you remember?' need not
preface.

There were times I remember fondly when I lay behind
rocks, bullets whizzing past my head. Cordite and dust
stinging my nostrils from impacts close enough to make
me nauseous. The concussion waves passed overhead in a
burst of hyper-charged molecules. The shockwaves
mushrooming out, rippling grass and sending the dust on
our vehicles two inches in the air.

What is crazy to me is that years after seeing and
participating in such an absurd way of life, I still catch
myself looking back and laughing, grimacing, and wanting
to vomit all over again. I look back at my combat
experience with grimaces, and at times late at night with
tears intermixed with laughter at the myriad situations I
genuinely enjoyed. While drinking with friends, we laugh
loudly at misfortunes and talk soft and intimate about
fights and dead men.

I watch movies, and I cry. When I do so, it all makes
more sense.

In the spring of 2005, third squad responded to the early
morning abduction of three Iraqi army soldiers from their

own base when we came under fire from two sides. The abduction took place in the early hours of the morning before the sun fully crept over the skyline of palms and flat-roofed buildings. Some smoke drifted lazily straight and wispy like thin yarn from the tandoori style ovens Iraqi women stoked pre-dawn. With no electricity, early mornings on post could have been the world hundreds of years ago before light pollution. It was a simple beauty I have not seen since, and I am afraid I will never see again.

The alarm blared. We, as QRF, lie fully clothed all night and jumped from bed, groggy, but quickly awake. Orison half ran into the squad area less than a minute after the initial wakeup while I pulled my flak jacket over my head and buckled it. I smacked a full magazine on my kevlar to seat the rounds fully against the metal—although I think this was more for confidence and show than to actually seat the ammunition. "What's going on?" was all I could manage in between the banging of my helmet. My body worked automatically after years of practice and real emergencies. I never thought about how to put the gear on in seconds. It just happened. We walked to the clearing barrels and forced magazines into the wells on the weapon's underside. My bolt was a little sticky. I'd have to clean it when we got back.

"Three Jundies were taken a bit ago from their beds and were seen headed north on Boston. We're going to try and get them back. Warmbier, radios up?"

"Yep, we're up." I was already in the vehicle and called a radio check to the COC. We had communication with our base, but not with the Jundies. This was normal and usually we talked with their handlers, a few army soldiers who lived with them. But this morning, I neglected to check their frequency, and we had no comms with them.

"Load up!" Orison called, almost unnecessarily, we performed these movements so often, there was no need for orders. Everyone knew their roles and carried them out automatically. The vehicles left the gate with no pomp, but simply dust and swiveling gun mounts.

I got on the radio and yelled over the whine of the revving engine. *Golf Four, this is Golf Four Delta. Any idea on where we will make contact? Over.*

Roger that Golf Four Bravo. This is Golf Four Actual (the lieutenant). Seems that some Jundies left in vehicles ahead of you and are trying to catch up. Be on your guard. Over.

As this was being relayed, we lumbered with four armored vehicles into the killing zone that developed between two fighting parties. The wheels crunched to a stop, as the vehicles veered in either direction down the line like a herringbone. The ricochets bounced all around my door and dug into the fiberglass hood of the Humvee with little pings and sharp thwacks.

"Holy dogshit!" Orison yelled to no one in particular. "Does anyone have a positive ID?" Through the six-inch square window of bullet-resistant glass, I searched the western side of the raised road. All I could see included a few small huts and the flashes from AK-47 muzzles.

"Fuck! Which side are our Judies on?" I was confused and frustrated. I know that all three of us in the vehicle, as well as all the other gunners in the other vehicles, were terrified of friendly fire incidents and hesitated, not wanting to open up on both the enemy and friendlies. Instead, they dropped behind turrets so we could establish ID. There is no good in fighting blindly if we did not have the identification of the real enemy. Marines are trained to make each shot matter. Each time we shot it was only for either suppression of a known enemy or aimed shots. Since we had no communication with the Jundies trying to save their friends, we had no idea which they were. Neither wore uniforms, and each side shot wildly, spraying everything with bullets. In retrospect, we should have powered through the fire, turned around in a line and established control of the battlefield instead of sitting like fools in the middle of it.

"Miles, which side should Barker open up on?"

After a few seconds of looking around, Orison yelled, "West side." I saw people pulling back into unmarked vehicles. I hoped he was right.

Barker was on the turret and slowly in a deep and plodding voice asked us, "Uh...Corporal, if I have a positive ID, can I shoot back?

We yelled back with a half bemused, half-frantic, "Christ, I don't care who you shoot anymore, just light 'em up!" and under my breath, "I am just sick of being shot at." I looked over at Orison and rolled my eyes, laughing.

On the west side beyond the rows of houses, along the street we would soon drive down, the enemy beheaded one of the police. They used a knife, and I thought it couldn't have been very sharp, because they sure made a mess of things. They thought it was fun to fire at us blundering down the road without comms with the Jundies, and on the other side, the Iraqi army who had completely broken firing at anything. Barker, a monstrous yet exceedingly gentle man who stood six and a half feet tall and, always smiling, showing large teeth, never opened up on anyone that day and I am thankful he didn't. We didn't have positive identification and were safe in the armored vehicles. Perhaps we provided a common target, an enemy they could both hate, and as the fire died down and the enemy drove away, the Jundies backed off too. We were left with the mess of the three captured and killed. But our presence was the reason it happened in the first place.

THERAPY

The Spartan office became more of a safety net, something to look forward to. My drives from Moscow to Spokane, a distance of some seventy miles each week became a meditation period. The drives home solidified as even more so.

She sat with her left leg crossed over her right at the knee. It was always this way. Always her legs over each other, hands rested on her left knee, eyes watchfully caressing my face. They were hard but also caring. "This may seem like a stupid question, but how do you think walking away from them as they boarded the bus changed your outlook on things?" She was referring to the third deployment, the one I missed out on. I am always relieved when the questions are less, "How does this make you feel?" and more "How has this changed you?" I am an English teacher. I can do analysis. I stared at her hands. They just sat there. They did not even tap. Her voice was deep and slow, it was a mother's soothing voice, it was honey, it was medicine I needed before talking.

"It certainly hurt, but to tell you the truth, I think more than anything else I did not feel needed anymore. For the rest of my time in the Marines, all three months of it, we had no purpose. We heard reports many mornings of attacks, wounded, killed and I knew most of their names. I drank with them, I trained them, these guys were everything to me. And now, there was no reason for me to still be in the Corps. I was, I am no good to anyone."

Glossary of Stuck Points #2: I am not needed, and if I am not needed, where is the purpose to be here?

She just sat there and smiled. "What you are telling me is nothing new and is something most vets who were in your position deal with. There usually is a feeling of being alone or not needed." Her voice suddenly switched tones. "This is a thought you cannot really listen to, Paul." She was more than serious. She was intent on passing on this last piece of help. It sounded afraid. "Paul, I would like to try something with you. That is, if you are interested. I think, personally, you could benefit from it, but I think it has become apparent you should try what we call 'cognitive behavioral therapy.'" I just raised my eyebrows causing her to stop abruptly. "I know, it sounds like I am going to pump you full of drugs, or Clockwork Orange you, but behavioral modification is not that at all. I do not want to alarm you, but from our previous conversations, and your stories, I think we are just touching the iceberg." Just touching the iceberg. That made me feel normal. I guess I realized I would not feel normal after going to a shrink, but this was more than I thought. Actually, I really did not know what to think about therapy, and how to talk to a shrink. I was just starting, and already she was panicking from my stories. When twenty-plus veterans commit suicide each day (statistically speaking), it made sense that therapists would recognize a cry for help when they saw it though. How did they sift through all the cries that came into their offices on a daily basis? Hell if I knew.

The problem is this: very few vets seem to take therapy seriously. If they attend voluntarily. No one wants to be the person weak enough to need therapy. Symptoms grow and do nothing to improve the quality of life. The mentality in the military is one where going to the doctor with broken bones is looked down on. They become "Sickbay Commandos" and everyone laughs at their attempts to take care of themselves. Some part of me knew I was already in that camp for going to therapy—if I told anyone I was going—and I was stuck there.

The next week I came back. She insisted I do so. She actually did not insist on words or actions, but her tone said it all. Therefore, I came early, sat in the chairs that made my back hurt, and waited.

"Good Morning, Paul, please follow me." She walked me to her office and gave me a clipboard. "Please fill this out to the best of your ability." You know the drill. I was beginning to, anyway. I hated this part. It was the necessary first step to any meeting. I thought it was too risky to be honest, but too transparent if I lied.

On a scale of 0 to 3, please rate the following.
(0 being very little with 3 being extreme)

Over the last week(s), how often have you been bothered by any of the following problems?

1. Little interest or pleasure in doing things	2
2. Feeling down, depressed, or hopeless	2
3. Trouble falling or staying asleep, or sleeping too much	3
4. Feeling tired or having little energy	3
5. Poor appetite or overeating	2
6. Feeling bad about yourself—or that you are a failure or have let yourself or your family down	2
7. Trouble concentrating on things, such as reading the newspaper or watching television	2
8. Moving or speaking so slowly that other people could have noticed. Or the opposite—being so fidgety or restless that you have been moving around a lot more than usual	2
9. Thoughts that you would be better off dead, or of hurting yourself in some way.	2

Please add the total #s 0-3 for all columns:	20

I took my time reading this and thinking through the checklist. How could I really give this my best analysis? For the whole week? I had good days and bad days, sure. Just sitting here looking at the sheet forced the color in my cheeks to rise. I huffed through each question and was a little disturbed when, in the end, my tally came to 20. Clearly, I was here for a reason.

"So, beyond the obvious, what is behavioral modification therapy?" I think I knew at the time she was on the verge of telling me.

At least I hoped so.

Personally, I didn't really see the point in embarking on something new without really knowing what was about to happen to my head.

"Well, that is a good question. Behavioral modification or other types of cognitive behavioral therapy are essentially as follows." She began to discuss the psychotherapeutic approach to identifying personal stuck points or thought triggers controlling what I was thinking about the world and those around me in everyday interactions. Apparently, through our conversations and notes from my other shrink, I shared classic signs of someone who needed to rethink basic aspects of human and interpersonal interactions. As well as talk through what was going on in my head.

We discussed the idea behind automatic thoughts we all have with each interaction and event and how the automatic thoughts, especially for someone who is traumatized, can illicit an undesirable emotion, often leading to a wrong or disproportionate extrapolation. In my case, apparently, I made it clear through my one-sided conversation that I was not thinking correctly about my everyday interactions and needed to change that. It revolved around one or more stories I told that bothered me. Stories I had a hard time resurrecting without difficulty, tears, and depression. However, those stories differed in their retelling. When I seemed to talk about them to my friends who had been there, they were not damaging, but to myself, they warped and twisted both me and the story themselves. This is classic. We were going to go over a structured program that was supposed to help me rethink how I think about these traumatic events, and how I can reshape my mental life out of it.

She explained how there are levels of cognitive processing. We all have "core beliefs." These reflect the ways we think about the world. They are usually unshakable and reflect our upbringing and larger family values. Beyond that are intermediate beliefs or "conditional assumptions." These assumptions are not as unshakable and helped to exacerbate my problem. They tend to encourage unrealistic standards for the real world. They just don't account for the unexpected events that we experience and the possible trauma we may encounter.

When core beliefs cause mental pain and torment from negative life experiences, we attempt to cope by creating compensatory strategies. When I am anxious or depressed, I engage in several possible strategies, I avoid behaviors so as not to aggravate the core belief, I oppose behaviors acted upon to prove the core belief is wrong, or I maintain support for the core belief. Personally, my favorite is to avoid it. It's just easier. Unfortunately, it is also fairly dangerous. That build-up got me in the end. And when it got me, I isolated myself.

So, here is the gist of stuck points and CBT as told by a layman. During traumatic events, and the aftermath of the storm, we develop glitches, or sticking points in our thought process that hinder the way we think. After the event and during natural interactions, our minds begin to alter the way we think, not believe, but think about the events and our lives in general. For example, I may have thought before that I was in Iraq for my friends and always would be. After all we had been through, it would be lunacy to think I would not be. However, a day comes along where they are caught in combat and I am back on the FOB. I can hear the firefight, and over the radio, intercept chatter. It is a frantic call for more ammunition. I begin to realize once again I cannot be there for them, not when they need us the most. How it makes me think about myself burrows in. I don't just feel awful remembering that, but begin to think that I am worthless and I begin to develop a stuck point. Over time I change the way I think about how reliable I am. Soon, I was to blame for the casualty, not simply just not there to help.

This is where CBT was supposed to come into play. Aided by a therapist, the traumatic event is teased out, and the resulting thought processes that related to the event are exposed through the examination of the traumatized by him/herself. The self-realization of the problem allows the person, guided by the therapist to begin to change the thought process or stuck point. I may feel like I am to blame for not being there for my friends, and that, therefore, I am a failure in other aspects of my life, but I can begin to start telling myself differently. Using a log and worksheets that contain leading questions, I begin to challenge how I think about said event and how I was actually not to blame, simply in the wrong place at the wrong time. Now, this paragraph seems to be a simple layer of stain over the bare grain of the problem; however, changing beliefs is not easy. CBT therapy contains weekly or biweekly meetings and the traumatized has to force himself to constantly be on guard against stuck points to identify and think through. Over time (mine was a twelve-week program) one can begin to change, but needless to say, accountability is not always there, and much like an addict, it is easy to relapse into dangerous thinking.

"Paul, through our new conversations relating to CBT, I want you to use this as a mantra, *I am perfectly imperfect*. Whenever you struggle and feel you are about to lose it, remember, we are all perfectly imperfect. Your core beliefs strengthened by conditional assumptions set you up for failure. They put the bar too high. But that is ok, no one is perfect."

She asked me to look over or memorize unhelpful thinking habits. I needed to be aware of ways I thought that were unhealthy or dangerous. I took the sheet in my sweaty hand and looked it over. "Next week I want you to share them with me and we can begin to address them, or at least prioritize them. I also want you to keep a written list of all stuck points you come across."

There were twelve boxes, one for each habit. The boxes included topics reminding me that I could not read others' minds and could not, therefore, assume what others think about me. Mental filters such as horse blinders let us only focus on certain harmful thoughts. Catastrophizing situations, which is a specialty of mine, always makes me think of the worst possible scenario and prepare for it. Comparing and despairing or seeing only the good in others while seeing nothing but bad in myself, was a real specialty of mine, although usually everyone is looked at in a critical light. There were others and reading through, I could see a bit of me in each. I am not sure that was good, or a stretch, but for the moment I noted it as being well rounded. Well-rounded is good, right? "And one last thing, Paul." She said this as an afterthought and seemed conflicted in the mention of it. "I would encourage you to get your stories down on paper. Tell them how they were, not how they become when you think about them too much."

A CHAPTER ON MARCHING

They usually started sometime around three in the morning. Well, to be honest, they started Thursday afternoons. Almost each Thursday afternoon, we would grumble for an hour or two while staring at a list of the gear the company commander would have assigned for each platoon to carry. As part of a heavy weapons platoon, I, and others, would be charged with carrying extra gear for the march. We would typically lay the gear out on our racks and the squad leader or platoon sergeant would stop by wearily to check it off before they would head home or back to their room to do the same. Traditionally, the load consisted of all the gear one would need to be combat-ready. A sleeping bag with bivy sack (a kind of heavyweight sleeping bag that was waterproof and the Marines' answer to the tent) extra sets of clothes, several canteens full of water (with gasmask drinking tubes that were always broken or missing), gas mask and filter canisters, individual first aid kit, flashlight, toiletries, weapons gear and combat load. This was different for each person. I favored having everything on an H-harness of suspenders that attached to a loose belt that held a dozen magazines in their pouches, a drop pouch for empty magazines for a firefight so if I fired several magazines I didn't lose them but could just drop them in this pouch to refill later. Flashlights. (because one inevitably didn't have batteries or some other problem only found when needed), grenade pouches, and a catch-all pouch that generally held food for short patrols. Some carried more magazines in-country than for marches back home where expediency was key. Some carried logs of dip, packs of cigarettes, or sunflower seeds.) We all wore a helmet and flak vest with SAPI plates in. The SAPI plates were the "bulletproof" ceramic and metal plates that were integral to the safety plan. They covered the person's upper chest to belly. We all carried rifles slung, but easily accessible because no matter how much we hated the forced marches, we all knew that we did them for a very good reason beyond conditioning.

After my first deployment, when I remembered the long marches we took to get to an objective, I took care to think of the marches as real training, even if I didn't know I took the care. Lastly, the weapons platoons carried their weapon systems. The machine gunners carried their heavy .50 caliber crew operated guns, the mortarmen, their mortar systems, we assaultmen, our SMAW rocket launchers. The mortars and machine gunners had it worse off than us assaultmen as they had about 150 pounds to spread around among three or four men, we only had twenty-four pounds on one person. The gear bounced around from person to person with the weapons occasionally leaving the squad for a fresh assaultman on the long marches.

We marched in file and column, and when one of our

platoons started to weaken and fall back, we went with him in ones and twos. Suffering is not equal in the Marines. I could always march well and power through by helping others regain their motivation and strength to rejoin the platoon. Having been a runner before the Marines, I was good at knowing how to mentally push through the pain of a heavy load and long miles marching. Many of the guys were short or didn't know how to distribute the weight, how to buckle the waste strap on the hips and adjust the shoulder straps to help keep the load centralized. There was no stopping, and those of us who could walked around and adjusted others' straps and gear on the march to help. We grabbed weapon systems off the backs of failing Marines, a .50 cal receiver thrown over the shoulder could do a world of benefit to that short Marine from the city who was trying in vain to ignore the pain as he slipped backward in the sand with each step forward.

The goal was to have no one fall out and be picked up by the trailing medics. To do so, we would grab packs and weapon systems, whatever was needed to lighten the load of the suffering. There were always a few mules that ended up with two full packs by the end of the march. In the march, the goal is everyone together, there are no individual personal bests, no rewards for being the toughest, you either finish, or you don't. In the desert of 29 Palms, the marches were brutal. Ten to fifteen miles through loose sand and jagged rock under a sun that is utterly unrelenting from the moment it breaks the skyline. Warm water, forced hydration stops, vomit in the sand, the stench of sweating out last night's vodka, inexperience, pain all took their tolls as at each stop there were a few dragging their back to the back, a medic beside them with his arm over their shoulder, walking them to the medic van. They were done. They failed.

A part of me loved them. In high school, our coach turned the rolling foothills and sage high desert of the Bitterroot mountain range into our training ground. We went on five to seven to ten mile runs at upwards of five to six thousand feet altitude, a bus dropping us off on a semi-deserted gravel road or thin trailhead, and we finished with our run when we got back to school. On those runs, I learned to separate myself from my body and just run, one foot in front of the other, just the sky, the sage, mountains, and me. I had no music—that being before reliable MP3 players even, only my thoughts in the desert and my mind trying to ignore the pain of my body.

The history of the military has a long relationship with forced marches going back to at least the Romans. As per the Roman writer, Vegetius, Roman army recruits were sent on forced marches to wean out the weak, but ultimately to show the recruits how far they can push their bodies before they break. It's an astonishing amount. For most of us, we don't really understand how far the body can be pushed, but what we know less of is how the mind can be pushed. For me, the marches were a time to be lost in my mind. I daydreamed of being back in the Idaho or Montana hills with a fly rod casting along a familiar stream. One foot pounded the dust and sand and the next while I was a thousand miles away.

I did the same while on patrols through the citrus groves and along mounded roads paralleling the Euphrates. I know I shouldn't have. I was supposed to be paying attention, but there had to be some moments when I was not there. At least in my head. To be present in the war was to risk losing the opportunity to remember who I was rather than who the war wanted me to become.

ALONE IN A CROWD
February 2004

Following the invasion of Iraq in 2003, we created a serious power vacuum. As the invasion units rotated back to the states, the military command, and men on the ground knew much more would be needed. While I was still in high school for the whole "Mission Accomplished" ceremony, everyone I talked to with experience, and every drill instructor and sergeant knew this would be a prolonged affair. My new battalion became one of the first to join the fight against the new insurgency cropping up. There were seeds of rebellion and anger sown overnight. Almost instantly, car bombs and anti-American sentiment grew to a boiling point. We went from liberators to occupiers overnight. There was no surprise when 2/7 deployed.

I think we were scared for very differing reasons. I think at first, in 2004, I was scared because I had no clue what was going to happen, and I think I was scared in 2005 because I did know what was going to happen, but I was constantly surprised. I was scared because I was eighteen, I was scared because I thought I would die, and

I was scared for what I thought and knew I would see and become.

Golf Company arrived near the Kuwaiti border mid-February 2004 and after a short stay where I rarely shut my eyes, struggling in the sun performing seemingly endless gun drills and mock patrols, and prepared for some unknown flight date, we got the word to get ready to go.

This was the main hub for all units going in and out of the Iraq theatre of war. We spent the time for the first few days camped out in Bedouin-style long tents. Thick cotton fabric stretched loosely over aluminum poles flapped in the wind while the kaleidoscopic fabric made me think of gypsy tents. I thought about how things here never really change in this world. Tradition is everything. We lived in replicas of the same tents Moses and Abraham camped in the same ones Saladin occupied when he took Jerusalem during the crusades. It was kind of enchanting, this new style of living, and when I would wake up in the morning, looking up at dusty geometric patterns, the fading colors illuminating the ridge of the canvas tents, and I almost always smiled to myself in spite of my newfound situation. The different colors played off my skin and dust, which began to cake on my white hands and face.

What happened those first few days are relatively unimportant to the story. We were new, and our clean clothes gave it away.

After a few days, I shuffled through the gaping back hatch of a C-130 cargo plane. There were no multicolored tiles in the spider's web of straps, ropes and exposed cables painting the walls of the inside of the aircraft. The C-130's really are amazing machines. Their payload is immense, and when pushed, Marines can stack in the back making it a veritable clown car. The flight was uneventful though the whole time I expected to bank sharply while taking evasive action, and within an hour or two of taking off, the loadmaster ordered us all to "stand up!" and "Move out of the back avoiding the propeller wash," which was actually quite impossible since the six-foot-tall propellers still swung round with enough velocity to make me stagger as I walked unsuspectingly through the hot wash.

The rest of the platoon joined us one morning with stories of their trip up. They all came tramping into our platoon area, stomping the dust off their boots looking like filthy and tired battle-hardened warriors. Their uniforms were salt-crusted and stained with the same dust that has stained warriors for many thousands of years. Their faces were turned into a harness of stone and stoicism that didn't fail to impress. I felt a little smaller and less important. I listened to their stories of security halts, smoke plumes and explosions, and a less-than-happy Iraqi populace. So far, the only real Iraqis I knew were the ones that pumped the shit out of the porta-potties that lined the walk outside our tents and were continually blowing over in the night winds.

I, for the first time, felt real jealousy that I was not part of this group suffering. The rest of the platoon seemed somehow more connected than I was with the. They had new jokes, and somehow being away from home wasn't as much of a tender point for most of them. I felt new and friendless like I was walking in on a conversation that was indiscreet and not for me. My squad was now filled with strangers who were vastly more experienced and I became diminutive.

Glossary of Stuck Points #3: When I am not there, bad things happen.

Now, since leaving the Marine Corps, I get that sick feeling in my stomach, and the knot won't go away; it feels sour and a bit like a hangover. In normal interactions with friends, my face flushes with shame and anxiety rises when I am not part of the group. Being part of a group is being at home and comfortable with the others. Without that, one is a lonely outcast. In the Marines, the team is everything.

In May 2007, my unit deployed for a third time to Iraq. Only a few of us remained behind. We shook their hands, and as they walked onto the bus, a little bit of me disappeared with them. It hurt not to go. I walked back to the barracks shuffling slightly with the few remaining friends. Slavens, who like me felt both relieved and terrible that we were not joining in, kicked rocks alongside. We were short-timers and would leave the Marines for good that June. We walked away and left our friends to their fate. It wasn't as if we could have changed the outcome or saved the men we trained. Some would die shortly after we left them. Others would come back changed, with new memories and new struggles I did not understand. I did not connect with the men who went on that third deployment, or the next one to Afghanistan. I simply no longer understood the struggles in the villages and deserts. I somehow grasped the importance of asinine problems back home. We maintained correspondence, but the *esprit de corps*—the unique connection Marines have who served together—it was missing. I did not go to their homecoming. A few traveled down but I didn't.

Just one minute about the strange process of removing oneself from the Marines. In retrospect, it is easy to laugh at this strange mentality. As one is recruited there is nothing more to life than the Marine lifestyle, tattoos, drinking, sex, fighting, and the strange motivation bordering on obsession. This obsession does not last too long for most people (especially for men who signed up for infantry) and in fact, most lose motivation before their first year has wrapped up. The Marine Corps is full of bullshit like if it were a vessel or bowl, bullshit would pile to the brim. Most bullshit involves mundane tasks such as watering pavement, raking gravel, polishing brass for hours at a time, or just "standing by to stand by." The latter is all-pervasive and if nothing else, encourages patience. If sitting on your backpack in formation waiting until 1400 for a bus that was supposed to take you out to training at 0600 doesn't build patience, nothing will. What it really does is make people super jaded. One bright spot of normalcy in this cavalcade of idiocy is the deployment. True, there is still a lot of standing by, but you get guns, and the prospect of shooting them at people (which is a prospect that intrigues a lot more people than would admit to it), and it lets one be with brothers and sisters of a like mind through troubling seas. Not being a part of that is devastating. When one is discharged, for a time, there is a relief. They escaped something hard and miserable, then there is understanding (usually around six months after EAS) that the rest of the world sucks, and they miss the freedom and acceptance of hedonism, and the brotherhood the Marine Corps provides. I am not entirely certain it isn't magic, but I am pretty confident it is brainwashing.

FIRST PATROL
March 2004
Al Baghdadi

I knew it had to come. I anticipated what I could, but no mental preparation can ever prepare a person for their first real combat patrol. In early March, once the whole platoon came together, and the army unit we relieved was just a vapor trail in the sky, the first patrol came. "Alright, boys, this is it." Armas's short frame and square jaw set in front of the squad; we, mostly new Marines, stood or sat in a semi-circle all around him. As he talked, he waved his open small green notebook containing the mission order. "Here is the patrol order. Everyone should fuckin' know all call-signs and contingencies, remember, you fuckin' boots, just like we fuckin' practiced over and over. Save all questions for the end, fuckin' got it?" He looked around us and us boots nodded and scribbled in our own notebooks. "Here is the situation. We are not anticipating an enemy, but keep your fuckin' eyes open and moving. The patrol will be after dark, so make sure you all have working NVGs as well as good mounts and extra batteries. If we do

encounter an enemy, you know the drill, return fire, establish fire superiority, identify the god-damn target, and assault in teams. Remember, violence of action. Assault the target and fuckin' kill the bastard so we can continue. But I don't expect any pussy ass enemy." He looked around studying all our faces for understanding and fear. "We roll through Al Baghdadi until we make our way to the old enlisted housing here." He tapped his finger down on a map he held. His finger landed north of town a kilometer or so. "Half of us will dismount and patrol beside the blacked-out vehicles. If you need to, use them for cover. We'll patrol through the housing area and head back. Keep your eyes peeled for the signs of IEDs and snipers."

After that, the briefs all became the same. We always had to look out for snipers, ambush points, and IEDs. "Warmbier, listen up, you fuckin' boot." My pen stopped scribbling. I looked up, confused. I was listening. Look out for snipers and IEDs, right? "Call signs. Get these down, Warmbier." This part was the nerve-wracking part. In combat, I was the radio operator and was expected to have an awareness of the situation, and as needed, walk-in airstrikes, adjust artillery fire, call in a casualty evacuation helicopter, and many other essential tasks while getting shot at, and potentially sustaining casualties.

Over the radio, we all had code names. Each entity operation on the battlefield, or behind the lines in an active support role, such as battalion or regiment, picked their own or at least officers picked their own in an attempt to feel more badass than they actually were. Battalion chose 'Wardogs' as their moniker. 2/7's official mascot was Cerberus, the three-headed dog who guards the entrance

of hades in Greek mythology. They also played off Shakespeare. Our unofficial battalion catchphrase was borrowed from Act three of *Julius Cesar,* "Cry Havoc and let loose the dogs of war." It was not uncommon during battalion level formations to hear someone yell "HAVOC!" from the middle of the formation. Golf Company chose the call sign 'Gunfighter,' making weapons platoon's second squad call sign Gunfighter Four Bravo. There were better ones out there too. Weapons company was 'Samurai,' the AC-130 support gunship overhead was 'slayer,' and General Mattis's personal call sign was 'chaos.' To the civilian, call signs are something silly, an attempt to sound better than we actually were, but to us, our call sign was an identity and carried loyalty.

Corporal Armas passed the call signs and their radio frequencies, and everyone wrote them down, in case I was wounded or killed. We passed out grenades and other explosives. The machine gunners stacked boxes of ammunition for their guns, something around a thousand rounds per gun, and we marched fully loaded to the vehicles. We must have looked a mixture of a sorry sight and like real killers. Each man carried two grenades, three hundred rounds of 5.56 ammunition; Slavens carried a thousand rounds for his M-240 and a thousand rounds for his M-249 SAW. We had our helmets and body armor, three liters of water per person, night vision gear, and a gas mask strapped to our thighs. Though we wore our gas masks at all times, we were not issued MOPP gear, so if a nerve agent were to be released near us, we would have been fucked regardless, but for some reason, command wanted us to wear the masks everywhere.

The sun began to set, and already only a glimmer of

the earlier rays fell below the ever-present desert floor which turned red in the fading light. The shadow of Armas pumped his fist up and down in the air dramatically, signaling to all drivers to start and begin to roll out. I sat in the bed of the first Humvee in line and looped the handle of the radio through my kevlar strap, keeping it on my ear.

Gunfighter, this is Gunfighter Four Bravo, requesting permission to step off, over. This was my first real radio transmission, and I stared at my squad leader, Corporal Armas, as I said it, desperate for approval. He nodded and called me 'a stupid fucking boot' under his breath while laughing. The reply to my call crackled over clear and crisp.

Gunfighter Four Bravo, this is Gunfighter, permission granted, out. It was that simple. I was expecting something long and arduous. I was expecting to fuck up, I was expecting, well, nothing less than total failure. What I got was impersonal but succinct approval. From here on out, I began to love acting as a radio operator.

We drove in line through the base at twenty miles an hour, closely packed. Driving past tents and rows of shipping containers, I looked out and saw men and women walking along the road looking up at us, our bristling porcupine of weapons, and I thought I saw jealousy and excitement. I was about to live what they wanted. A few called out to us, "Get some!" or "Oorah!" and we smiled and held our weapons closer and drove on.

We passed through the gates of the base, and the world seemed a bit darker. The gates glowed with dozens of high-power floodlights, and beyond the light seemed dead and cold and barren. I caught the outlines of burned-out

tanks and troop carriers from the invasion and imagined ghosts watching us in the lumps of blackened iron.

The convoy kept fifty to one-hundred-meter dispersion between vehicles, and we made the turn from the main MSR through Baghdadi to the beginning of our patrol route. My heart pumped hard, and I felt the blood in my ears. The air was beginning to chill in the night air. We slowed through the village. My heart pumped harder when I saw all the people out on the streets. Little kids ran everywhere, playing with soccer balls and stopping to wave at us and gather close to the vehicles. Their parents grabbed them and scuttled off to a safe distance from these new uniforms and guns glaring down at them. Marines are trained from day one to meet every action with force and aggression, and we immediately assumed a protective posture around our vehicles shouting at all who we thought walked too close to the slow trucks.

I did not expect to see all the kids. What if I accidentally dropped one of them? Would I ever be able to live with myself? Would I be able to live with myself if I killed any of these people? They didn't seem like the killers I was expecting, but like fathers and mothers, kids, grandparents, and neighbors I grew up with. The sun dropped down beyond the horizon, and the last rays kicked up the few remaining heat waves radiating up from the metal and fiberglass of the Humvee. "Warmbier, hey, Warmbier!" My team leader was staring intently at me.

"Yes, Lance Corporal?" my voice shook and betrayed all the nervousness I felt since the airplane lifted its gears in California. I was surprised I could make noise at all.

"Chill, just stay on your toes." He smiled, and I knew I was supposed to feel better, but I was worlds away. My nerves were a sinking ship. It was inevitable. There was no saving this one. We slowed and the silence following the Humvees stopping was almost instantly shattered as something came from the darkness howling. A street dog. Feral street dogs were a real problem in Iraq and caused innumerable patrols to hesitate out of surprise. Later on, we would shoot any feral dog packs we found. "Holy Mother of God! Fucking shit!" Armas yelled as the dog barked and yowled feet from his door, taking him totally by surprise.

I would like to say that I calmed down and operated as a professional should, but the whole drive to our drop off point I was skittish. We drove through Al Baghdadi and north to the compound that was our foot patrol. We dismounted. "Warmbier, I'm taking point, you on my right, Hoover is on my left." Armas' quick orders hissed through the still air. We walked through the gates of the block of houses making up the former military compound. Everything was black. The vehicles followed our front rank of the three of us. Walking beside the vehicles a little ways off, but close enough to use them as cover walked the remainder of the squad. We walked erect and tall, our fingers hovering over the trigger guard, our eyes darting back and forth behind the green glow of night-vision goggles. My fingers trembled slightly.

What would happen if we were attacked? I knew my SOPs pretty well, but how would I respond to a firefight? I had no idea, and that terrified me. Would I find cover fast enough and simply cower while others fought? Would I be dropped in the initial ambush that was sure to follow? Or would I do what I had been trained to do without thinking and press the attack, do what Marines do better than any force in the world, and simply move into the fire and overwhelm the enemy?

Movement. Time passed and the tension ebbed.

Just a dog. I saw it dash through an alley from the corner of my field of view, and immediately my weapon came up, my finger feathering the safety. "Warmbier, whatcha got?" Armas was suddenly beside me, crouching and pulling my frame down forcefully from the shoulder.

"Not sure, Corporal, I think it was just a dog. Probably the same fucker as before."

"Ok, stay alert." He patted my shoulder and stood to move forward again, the low growl of the Humvee following. I lingered for only a moment more and stood to follow.

We had a sniper team with us and Armas, spotting an old and demolished cafeteria to the right, motioned for them to dismount and help clear the building. The snipers consisted of two teams and two sniper weapons; the other two men had M-16s with M-203 grenade launchers mounted under the barrel. They jumped out and the Humvees turned off for a moment while the five cleared the building. I punched out a few meters to the left to provide security and hunkered down beside a crumbling cinder block wall. Resting my hand on the cold stone, my fingers found evidence of former fights. My fingers fit easily into the holes, and blindly my hand groped the holes as my head swiveled behind the goggles, eyes wide open, waiting for the ambush. I leaned down and peered through the hole, a streetlight glaring through the bullet's path. Glass crunched under the silent raiders as they moved room to room clearing the building. Low murmuring issued from men beyond and away. Not in the world of my night vision, they were miles away and consisted of nothing but disembodied voices in my heightened adrenaline-fueled hearing. Closer, the crackle of the radio echoed off the walled compound and sounded like a loudspeaker. *Gunfighter Four Bravo, this is Gunfighter. Gunfighter actual requests an immediate sit rep, how copy?*

Roger, stand by for sit rep. The unrecognizable team leader's voice, soft and controlled. How could he be so calm? Did he know something I didn't about our chances of combat that night? *Gunfighter we are at grid 5-6-7-4-3-4-9-6. Break. We have dismounted and are clearing a building for an observation post. How copy?*

Roger, solid copy. The crunching came back. I turned around and saw Armas and the others slowly plodding through the black doorway where my goggles could not penetrate. After the sound, they simply appeared calm, confident. He silently motioned for us to stand, raising his palm up, and followed with a forward motion. I stood, glad to move again, and with a little more confidence moved forward, eyes down every alleyway, scrutinizing each bag of trash, desperately peering into the black of open windows, looking for the glint of a barrel in the shadows. My weapon was up and in my shoulder constantly.

We walked slowly, plodding beside the growling vehicles, tripping over invisible rocks. We reached the end of the road and a pair of gates looking out to the MSR. The whole patrol only took perhaps an hour, but time morphed and slowed as we moved and stopped and moved again at every potential movement. Suddenly Armas raised a fist and ran back to the Humvee. He spoke to a sniper who raised his weapon slowly and took his time. I took a knee and he came to me. "Warmbier. There is a fucking guy on the road a hundred meters up or so. He has an AK. We're moving forward and are going to flash him with the lights before lighting him up. He may be ICDC. Or he may be a bad guy. Be ready to light him up." I swallowed and nodded, trying to say something to the affirmative. And stuck with the nod. I saw him too suddenly. He stood on the road, AK held in one hand, cigarette in the other continually moving to his lips and back in a quick movement. Armas had another word with the sniper, and I raised my weapon as he did. He counted from three and the brights on the Humvee flashed like the sun. The man surprised just stood there, staring at the lights. My finger flicked the safety to "Burst," and my finger rested on the trigger.

"Stand down!" he yelled, suddenly panic in the high voice. The safety flicked back to "Safe," and I lowered it recognizing why he did so. The man wore cammies and a patch that read clearly in the light, ICDC. The lights flicked again, and I dropped once more into a black world. My night sight went. It would take a minute or two to adjust. "Christ, I almost zipped him," Armas was saying in the cab of the Humvee. He just kept repeating it. "Almost zipped him." I too almost put a couple rounds through his body.

Our first patrol and we already inadvertently attempted to bring down the fledgling Iraqi defense force. The man disappeared off the road, and I never saw him again. In the darkness and over the rumble of engines, laughter. Simply nervous laughter.

THE SICKNESS
Al Anbar, Iraq
2004-2005

<u>Glossary of Stuck Points # 4:</u> I let my body succumb to sickness. Succumbing to anything leads to utter failure.

The shitters were dangerous enough on their own, bringing disease and threatening to make men pass out when a strong breeze came. It may have been over a hundred outside, but it was at least twenty to thirty degrees hotter in the plastic death shitters. Most men timed their needs for nighttime, but well, when you have to go. Almost immediately, the smells begat flies and the flies brought sickness making a terrible cycle.

"Wash your god damned nasty mitts!" the Company First Sergeant screamed at us shortly after we all rejoined as a company. "Drink your water, and wash your damned hands after wiping your ass!" I stood in the back of the company formation, swaying slightly. I was sick.

The flies landed on the food, on our faces, on our shit,

on everything. There was no way out of it. Within a couple of weeks, most of us brought bottles of water into the bathrooms so we could rehydrate while in the horrible sauna. I stood in the back and went over in my mind how in the world I could have gotten sick already. I used hand sanitizer, almost constantly dumping it into my palm as if it were gold, made sure there were a minimum number of flies on my food and didn't eat the local food. I still became sick and tried to hide it so I would still be able to go on patrols. I was lucky. I heard rumors of men writing home asking for Depends diapers from their families so shitting themselves on patrol became less of a chore. I did write home. I wrote to my parents in one of my very rare letters and asked my mom to have my grandparents send Depends.

A month later, I picked up a box from my grandma. Inside was a letter and a smattering of odd items. There was a pack of hot chocolate (because there is nothing better than drinking hot chocolate in one-hundred-degree heat), a box of tampons, and a box of panty liners. There was a note too.

Dear Paul,
Your dad mentioned you wanted diapers. I thought these would be more useful. I heard from one of my old friends at church here say that I should send tampons. You can plug bullet holes with them. She also said the panty liners would be great in your helmet to absorb sweat from your head. Isn't she so smart?
Love, Grandma

No. There was no way. I sat in stunned disbelief for

probably five minutes. Tampons and super absorbent panty liners. Responding to my frozen body, a few came over and peered into my box. "No way. Who sent these?" Armas picked up the box and barked out a laugh calling others over. "Warmbier has tampons and period paper! I always knew you were a pussy, Warmbier." Later, I slipped a tampon through the loops of my flak vest, just in case.

No one teased one another about the sickness. One morning, early on, our lieutenant called all thirty of us over to him so he could give us information about future patrols, problems in the platoon, and other news. "Ok, Devils, out here, men will shit themselves. It may be during combat, it may be from sickness, I do not want to hear one fucking word about teasing. Any one of you could be in the same boat at any time, understand?" we all nodded, some trying to hold back chuckles or smiles. "I fucking mean it, gents. If someone is sick, help them out." We waited for the rest of the news. From out of one of the tents down the row, a Marine wearing nothing but green issued running shorts and holding in one hand a box of baby wipes, and in the other, his rifle sprinted by the platoon. He ran into one of the shitters, making an audible groan as he presumably didn't make it in time.

On my second deployment, there was more of an issue with sickness. In fact, the issue was more dangerous, as well as more intense. On the first deployment, most of the patrols were in vehicles, driving through the desert, or down some road searching for IEDs. When someone was sick, they just lay on the floor of the vehicle and moaned.

Later we were deployed to an FOB (forward operating base) on the southwest section of Fallujah city. All patrols began and ended as foot mobile patrols. The platoons were shorthanded most of the time, and the shits did not qualify to disqualify someone from patrol. It was always easy to spot them. The sick ones walked out of the platoon buildings with slumped shoulders as if the whole weight of the misery of existence were dropped right on them. Their eyes studied the ground, not strong enough to look up at anyone, and the gear, dropped to the bare minimum, seemed to crush them like medieval pressing punishment. Occasionally, their eyes looked up panicked and a little weary, and they rushed back through the doors to emerge later wearing new pants.

This happened to me a few times, and at its worst, I lay hardly able to move on the balcony outside the main room. I wore no blanket and only underwear. My body would hardly respond and only would do so by shitting when I went vertical. I lay on rubble and heavily used porn magazines, a strange woman's paper thighs cradling my head. Occasionally, I shuffled sideways so someone else could use the shitter tent, usually in a panic, usually asking if there was room for another next to me on my porn bed. "No, do your business and leave me alone." I croaked, hardly any strength to talk. The only strength I had I saved for drinking water. The night was warm and a soft breeze caressed my goose-bumped skin. *I am going to die here. Like some homeless person sleeping on newspaper. Why the fuck did I sign that contract?* The thoughts went in and out of my head as the hours passed. I listened to cars pass all night. Birds wheeled overhead, the movement of air the only indication of their feeding. Every few minutes, explosions far off and close echoed off my prison walls. Once, one blew close enough to shake the gossamer fabric of the tent shitter. Bursts of AK fire chattered back and forth like bickering couples. The next day, men geared up for patrol. I struggled up, unwilling to be left behind. They left me behind. I lay all day on my rack sweating and shitting. How I didn't shrivel up like a raisin, I have no clue, here is the deal though, the whole time I waited for the explosions that would trigger guilt. I knew I was going to miss out on all the action, and more pressingly, they would need me. I was the radio operator and although my replacement knew what he was doing, I knew I had more experience. No one died, no attack came, and I escaped. But while the squad walked the streets looking for snipers, I drowned. I lay there in self-pity and loathing. I let them down. I could never repay the days I missed patrols.

The patrol base consisted of four buildings. All stood three stories and used to hold beautiful tile floors, chandeliers of bronze, and velvet furniture. The compound became a base shortly after the Second Battle of Fallujah and Marines quickly erected posts and established a command post in one of the nicest buildings. The compound was walled off from the world, and the Marines reinforced the buildings with countless sandbags stacked sometimes four deep to keep out sniper's bullets and RPG rounds. In the west of the compound, second and third platoons lived in a building each. In a small corner smoldered a communal burn pit whose flame and smoke and snow of ash was constant. Into this went half-eaten MRE packets, sealed plastic bags full of piss and shit soaking into grey beads, leftover wood, and whatever evidence of shenanigans needing secretly destroyed in a hurry. On the east side was weapon platoon's building and standing strong and impenetrable, the command building where first platoon had a few small rooms. This building was the staging area for patrols as well as for Catholic mass and Protestant services when the chaplains made their rounds. A single long table stretched out luxuriously on the porch of the command building. This table held many things over time.

When the chow truck came bringing hot dinner, a respite from MREs, the food spread out on the table, vats of rice, turkey, boiled beef, steamed vegetables, and other treats. When the platoon on patrol unearthed a weapons cache, most of the explosives and guns were loaded on a truck and brought to the table in order to be cataloged and to leave rust flakes and filth before it was taken out of town where it evaporated into black smoke and iron fragments.

When the wounded came to the base, they were laid gently on the table for the medics to work on. Their blood poured from their wounds and sunk deeply into the wood, bringing out the natural grain and coloring it deep rust. Hours later, the food trays plopped down on the newly stained wood, and the flies greedily feasted before making their way back to us. Because of this, the sickness stayed with us and many keep it still.

BLOOD AND DUST
Fallujah 2005

It hit the vehicle with the jarring finality of a landslide. On my second deployment, while stationed inside Fallujah, a vehicle-borne IED exploded next to the side of my platoon sergeant's truck. Five men poured blood, muscle, bone from their bodies. Gunn Dobbins lost chunks of his neck and triceps. Doc Hu, our corpsman who studied anatomy books in the squad area and then yelled at Iraqis in Mandarin, had various pieces of his face ripped off violently by shrapnel. Seeing him after the deployment was in stark contrast to the way I left him before he lay closed eyes, almost corpselike, gushing blood and fatty chunks visible from a ripped and destroyed mouth. Now, only a little scar shows from his cheek to his mouth, the only physical reminder of a nightmare. Murray—a loud and round-headed man with an opinion for everything and a predilection to fight for any reason— took arguably the brunt of the blast and unluckily enough lost much of his skull. His grey and red-streaked brains visible and pulsating. The vehicle returned to base and the frantic corpsmen fell onto the lot.

Wilkins now goes by the moniker of "One-Eyed Willy" for a reason. The funny thing about Wilkins' injury is that he was wearing ballistic Oakley glasses. Our command at the time viewed ballistic Oakley sunglasses as strongest and best. I owned a few pairs myself over the years and found them to be damn tough. In training once, I even put a pair a mere foot directly front and center to a claymore mine. Not a single baring scratched the lenses, though the frame evaporated. I guess no matter what you wear if a two-inch long piece of jagged steel wants to puncture your face, it will find a way through. I believe Willy still has the glasses that popped his eyeball like a stepped-on grape; personally, I hope the iron shard is still embedded in ballistic matched, bomb-proof lenses.

Bennet had his hand hanging out of the vehicle door. He was in the front seat and had the tip of one of his fingers torn off.

Little Villasana. Villasana was a Mexican-American Marine and, most of the time, 'talked' in an intelligible mumble somewhere between Spanish, English, and I think Vietnamese. We dubbed his language Villasaneese and simply assumed there was no way we would ever understand his ramblings. The Spanish speakers struggled just as much as the English with his mumbles. He was caught under the chin by a piece of shrapnel so luckily placed that it scratched him deep, drawing blood, but well enough to earn him with a purple heart. Villasana responded. All the men poured blood all over the back of the vehicle, turning it into a cauldron of flesh and bone. Smithy and Villasana became medical wizards. Most likely, they saved the lives of the wounded. Villasana was given an award—the Naval Achievement Medal (or NAM) with valor distinguishing device.

Glossary of Stuck Points #5: I was not there, I should have been, I could have helped. I let them down.

These men have been bothering me for now over eight years. It keeps me up at night, it keeps me from smiling at day, and compounded to other events becomes my survivor's guilt. It comes and goes to some traumatized individuals manifesting itself, like all PTSD, differently in the affected. Some never become affected by the guilt that plagues others. Even though all ended up surviving, and Gunny Dobbins found time and energy to flip off our company first sergeant as he was loaded into the ambulance.

The cauldron of blood was my vehicle.

Up until the time of departure, I had squeezed myself onto the bench beside Dobbins and Murray, but at the last minute, Dobbins pointed one finger out of the vehicle and smiled. He was being generous, keeping me from a long patrol for a ten-minute radio operator's job. He wanted me to do a communications handover. He most likely saved my life.

I heard the explosion from miles away and knew. Unlike the explosion that killed eleven Echo Company Marines, I more felt than heard the explosion tear through their bodies and ran with Cpl. Tobin (with whom I was performing the comms handover, and who incidentally was killed a year or so after being discharged from the Marines; I got the phone call from several of my buddies after work in April and wept for an hour in my car before being able to drive home) to the roof of our FOB. We looked at each other and, for a moment, shared the look. Our world changed, and I knew something disastrous happened as the black plume billowed up and upon itself to the sky off in the distance. I knew and was not surprised when the convoy screeched to a halt into the Forward Operating Base. All five vehicles drove in. One I could see from the rooftop more limped in than drove. Several of the tires were shredded and ran only on their internal run-flat-tire. The thin armor on the sides pockmarked, and anything that was not metal was shredded and hung limp. The vehicle, now it made the mad dash to base collapsed and spluttered to a halt. It seemed to sink lower in the sand as the engine halted. And the medical team converged on my late truck with an urgency I was not used to seeing.

I saw the men loaded on the vehicle tripping on morphine and still bleeding through their bandages. Knew then that I should have been with them. Wanting to be wounded is admittedly a very strange feeling to have, but remnants of it have stayed with me. They sit under the skin and occasionally poke out and show, usually at the worst time. I dream of it, wake up remembering wanting with everything in me to have taken some of the brunt of war with them, instead of them, for them. I should have let my blood mingle with theirs, and I should have suffered as was my place to do so.

It is interesting that many people, when they realize they have done the wrong thing, said the wrong thing or otherwise offended propriety, fate, or anything else immediately try to make amends or secure their penance from the offset. I think for many of us, it is something we never really outgrow as the last vestige of childhood guilt, and for me, I hope it is something I never outgrow. Maybe it's because I grew up and maintain my Lutheran ideals and was used to reciting that I am a wretched creature needing help. I knew that my penance was to throw myself into work. Immediately I ran from the rooftop at a breakneck speed and found work to do.

I barreled down the stairs and into the courtyard and into the knot of wide-eyed brothers I would have given my life for, failed to give my life for. The medics stood around, the ambulance just skidding off down the road with a new escort of vehicles. When I opened the vehicle's back hatch, I was met with a deluge of bandages, congealing blood and flesh that still dripped from the benches and down the sides of the armor to mingle and coagulate together. A single hand print in red stood out on the gate, no dripping, no horror movie theatrics, only a hand print like ancient aboriginal art on a cave wall

Magallion, a short deeply sarcastic Marine and one of my best friends during those years, helped me pour water and sweep, liter by liter and stroke by stroke over the bed of the truck until it was all out. The water fell out of the thin bottleneck of the half-closed gate as we pushed it, our boot soles staining red and becoming slippery in the pools of our friends. Each blob of water met with blood and flesh and urged it toward the gate. Some pieces did not want to go and took a finger or broom handle to coax them out. More often than not, we employed the broom and swooshed the viscera out. In minutes, my boots, pants and hands shone maroon and brown. We did not look at each other while we worked. It would have destroyed us to share this with another soul till it was done. Silently we poured water, threw empty bottles over the side, brushed the floor and retreated deep into some part of ourselves that didn't have to process what was going on. This certainly wasn't the worst war had to offer, but there was something different about the blood of brothers rather than that of enemies that sets off little bombs in someone. It was something that was actively destroying the last vestiges I contained of care for the war, justification for our cause, desire to be there. As we washed away the blood, we washed ourselves of any last bit of innocence in a baptism of horror.

Our Company First Sergeant saw the mess and shooed us away, "Go and help your brothers. Take a break." His eyes behind thick glasses shone with tears held back and his set jaw betrayed horror at what we were doing. We shuffled over half in a daze, hands dripping, permanent fingerprint stains embedded in the grain of our trousers.

Halfway to the platoon area where we could just hear muted and hushed voices, a lieutenant, a man we nicknamed "Seventh Cav" during training after Gen. Custer for his inability to keep our platoon alive in training scenarios—Seventh Cav called the two of us over. His smooth hands rested on his wide hips, and a sneering smile lingered on his twenty-two-year-old face. "Now," he paused, his high pitched nasally whine and Texas twang twisted the knife. "You boys know you won't get out of your patrol for today, right?" Hardly listening, not even registering the question, we answered.

"Yes, Sir." We muttered in unison. We tried to move past, but he blocked our way, sneering.

"Do you understand me, Marines? Go finish cleaning

your gear, and get ready for patrol." We stopped and looked at each other. I could not believe what I heard and looked over at Magallion for support, but he betrayed nothing. He really wanted us to clean the gear? Our company Gunnery Sergeant, heard all this and disengaged himself from talking with the First Sergeant.

"Ok, Sir, I'll take care of these two. Let's go, Warmbier, Magallion." He took us by the shoulders and away from the sneering officer. His voice was soft and comforting, "You two eat and rest, you are not going on any patrol until you rest." Eat. Like anything would look good for a long time. What could I eat that didn't remind me of the steaming stew in the back of the vehicle?

In the platoon area, the three squads sat in small groups on the stairs. Their hands moved slowly and delicately. Their eyes were dark, and shoulders hunched over weapons. At their feet, strips of bloody gauze and cleaning patches littered the stairs. They were picking bits of bone, muscle and semi-congealed blood off the weapons. Magallion sat down and mechanically took hold of an untouched weapon splattered brown and red. Choking down the rising fear and pain, I began to sit. "We have it covered, Warmbier, but I think they need help scrubbing the flaks." The voice was hard and deep. It was cut off from emotion. I don't remember who owned it, but I walked behind the building where a bucket of deeply tinted water stood, Tobin's arms up to the elbow in the water. Seeing me, he took them out and the red dripped slow and glutinous on the ground. The blood lingered on his fingers for just a brief moment before sliding to the ground.

"You going to relieve me?"

"Yeah, take a break." Both voices betrayed men on the brink of collapse. I emptied the tub, and fifty gallons of bloody water sloshed over my boots and pant legs into a pool slowly filtering through the sand. The tub filled up. Grabbing the large flak Gunny Dobbins used to own, plunged my arms deep in the water. I grabbed a scrub brush, and the water went from pink to red rust as I scrubbed harder and faster, my emotions coming back. Each time I took the flak out of the water, I hoped the blood would disappear. Each time, my arms tinged a deeper shade of fuchsia. Each time the blood dripped thinner off my hands.

We were part of a company whose commander told us at the end of the deployment that PTSD was all made up bullshit, and "You had better not make out that you have it to get out of patrols or deployments!" So, this was, in a way, par for the course.

The reason for the patrol had been to pick up a working dog-handler and take her and her German Shepard to a vehicle checkpoint where the two of them would commence in terrorizing the inhabitants for several days. She and her dog had been in a different vehicle during the blast, and while we were cleaning the gear, I heard her tell whomever she was walking with "Why the fuck are they cleaning that? And why the fuck are they so calm about it?" The panic cut in her voice, and as she went on, her voice became hoarse and finally broke at the end as it collapsed.

Uncontrollable grief and disbelief washed over me in a wave of blood and fear. I wept angry and bitter tears, my body shivering and shaking with each breath not fully taken. The images flashed over and again in my mind. The blood dripping off the seats, bits of flesh splashed down in a squelching plop. Even still, even though no Marines died that day, I think what I dwell on more than anything else is what I avoided.

Later in the afternoon, we did go on that patrol. Our Sergeant making it happen to give us something to keep our minds off the morning. He went to us all to tell us individually. I sat against the wall surrounding the roof of our barracks building. I slumped with my face on my knees, no more water for tears. I sat there lost. My hands shook, and my brain quivered from the onslaught of memories. Were they alive? All of them? What if someone died? I was supposed to be there, right next to Dobbins. The piece of metal that tore his neck and tricep into ribbons would have cleaved the back of my skull. And here I was, alive, unscarred and they lay on cots in the belly of a plane headed for Germany with a morphine drip. The air within the plane would be filled with groans, screams, and a smell of isopropyl alcohol and flesh perpetually hanging there, mingling with the exhaust from the engines. The Sergeant came up to me and knelt down. "Warmbier." His voice sounded hard and forced. "Warmbier, gear up. You are coming on the foot patrol. You need to get out of here." He stood and turned back to me after a step or two. "Common, let's go Marine. With any luck, we can get into a fight and kill the motherfuckers who are responsible. Or any motherfucker at all."

With that, I got up and slung my gear over my head.

THERAPY

Glossary of stuck points #6: When I fail, at anything at all, I am worthless, people die because of failure. When I fail, people die. When something is not done right the first time, I fail.

I know the therapist has heard it all. I know that my story is not really that interesting or exciting as far as war stories are concerned. I also know deep inside that my story cannot be judged by an outside observer. I know that is not her goal, and that she simply wants to help me make sense of it all.

"Thank you for sharing with me, Paul." Her words are slow to come out, and it is clear she wants me to know she is sincere. I have a small pile of tissues in my lap. This is usually how it goes. I can tell this story without tears, but when I am in a shrink's office, the waterworks come hard and fast. But the strangest thing is this - I don't feel like a little bitch when crying. Years ago, in the Marines, that would have been a different story. I had a dream the night before. My dead friends were there, the suicide and combat dead. Somehow, I couldn't talk to them and tried so hard. There was no getting over this. She was usually just interested in the here and now and not my subconscious but listened quietly nonetheless. She liked to humor me. It bothered and frightened me. I shook when I talked about it. I shook the whole way up that morning.

"Paul, what do you make of this in regard to your emotional stuck points? It is clear to me that, like many other veterans, the emotional aspects of life are easier to set you off." She told me she saw too often when veterans come in and were so used to turning off emotions that we had to pry them open almost by force. "I am glad you have told me these stories, and I hope next time we can talk about more of them." Her voice was clear and steady. In the meantime, Marla gave me more homework. I was supposed to start writing down each time I felt emotionally aroused by something, reminding me of Iraq. I was to write them down and think about what caused them and talk about them next time. "I don't want you to avoid these situations like we all want to do," but I was to let them come organically. Later we can sit down together and analyze what is possibly going on."

I experience many different emotional triggers from time to time, as we all do. There are days I don't leave the house. I simply can't. I try. What is it that stops me? Shortly after my discharge, I began to feel a detachment from people. There were and still are very few I care to be around. It is not that I dislike their personalities, but I cannot relate easily. That has lessened over the years as my identity has shifted from Marine to writer, teacher, person. I cannot sit down with someone and engage in small talk easily. The thought of having to do so drives me wild and somehow brings an irrational fear to the cocktail of emotions I am already feeling. I struggle enough with my own internal (and occasionally external) dialogues, why would I want to add more noise?

I feel stuck between dimensions like I'm in two worlds at once and I am continually waiting for Rod Sterling to come out and narrate. How can I find my way home when I have left it, never to come back, a bombed-out shell of a palace? How will I sleep at night without my M-16 tight? Had I become married to my former profession forever, a ghost of my present self, or is this just my life now? If given this opportunity again, would I take it? Was there something I could have done to keep Dobbins, Wilkins, Funke, Stevens, Martinez, Tinsley, Walker, Tobin, Hunt, and many, many others—whose names I am ashamed to say dance out of my reach—from death or injury? Why do I still occasionally swerve into the other lane when I drive past trash in the barrow pits? Do I still have family, or are they buried, their memories covered forever, drowning in the shifting sands? Will I ever recognize myself again? Moreover, why on earth am I sharing this with a shrink? Am I so weak that I need to pour out my petty problems to someone I barely know? I feel like a toddler just learning to talk. I babble out loud and my mouth runs a million words a minute.

Upstairs, I'm still over there. I'm afraid I'll always be over there.

She interjects to remind me that I'm not still there and that *I can come home anytime I want.* But the few times when I have been 'home' and I see my friends from high school, why do they not recognize me, but walk past? When I track them down and begin to talk, why do they want to get away so quickly? Have I changed that much?

Maybe I have changed that much, and sadly won't be able to relate to many of my old friends anymore. There is hope, I guess.

Problem: do I even want any part of that last life?

Answer: no, not really.

"Paul, what is a stuck point?" I held the sheet in my hand, where my hand was, my sweat crinkled the paper slightly, and on the freshly printed page, the ink ran slightly, sliding down the page and terminating at the next words. I sat on a cheap IKEA couch with grey woven fabric and kept my head down as the bile rose in my stomach and my voice broke.

"Stuck points are automatic thoughts that keep me from recovering. They are thoughts that come after actions that are a hindrance to thinking differently." She nodded.

"Good, and what are not stuck points?" the room was stifling. At this part of the session, roughly halfway through, it always felt stifling. Outside the window I had my back to, the snow drifted down lazy and slow. The flakes fell, unencumbered by anything, even gravity seemed to not weigh them down. They were without worry, nothing stuck them from doing exactly what they were supposed to do. The flakes drifted onto cars, roads, and below me two stories, an old and hunched man. I noticed him when I first walked in, and he just sat there, smoking, allowing the snow to turn him into a drift. Even in this place of revelations and personal depth, we sit and wait for the snow to cover us and hide us from the world.

"Stuck points are not behaviors, feelings, facts, questions or moral statements." I read aloud. "They are only thoughts." And according to this sheet, thoughts can be changed.

"But they can only be changed if you want them to, and if you put in the work." She admonished me as I am sure she had done to countless others in my chair. But she was right, did I want to change my thoughts? Was I simply there to tell stories and find some magic pill that didn't exist? Was I only there because I knew I needed to be? I couldn't help but tell my stories. They were so important to me, I couldn't see a way to break them away. They were what made me different, special, they were what made me see the world how I did. They have always held me back though. They have always been the pillar that allowed me to walk straight and tall. Maybe, if I could just tell them once more and then cease, I could release their power.

The power they held over me was one of plastic like flexicuffs that have been banded around my body over and over and zipped tight so I could only move and never break. I wriggled and groaned as the ambiguous and invisible bonds held me tight.

The power is incredible, it is the memory of zip-tying others, of slipping sandbags over children's' heads so they do not see and tying parents up so we can take them away and they can disappear as we move to the next house.

What are these guns doing here!

Why do you have artillery rounds!?

How do you say 'you're fucked' in Arabic?

As crying children softly whimper and sniffle in the dark corners of their prayer room, children the same age as mine now, children for whom I know I would burn the world to cinders if anyone, government or not, came and harmed them.

The situations have flipped, I am in bondage through

my stories and I want release, I scream for a way to remove the sandbag but the memories hold me tight, iron muzzle break held against my skin yelling in my mind as my wife and children bear the burden of memory for me. But as I leave the therapy room, she tells me there is an escape, I remember her voice sifting through the haze of tears and blanket of guilt, there is a way out that is productive. I know I will never release the feeling of guilt, but I can harness it, use it, embrace it to do something better, to build rather than destroy. But the stories keep coming.

FERRIS TOWN
Al Anbar Province
March-April 2004

Night vision goggles don't often absorb enough light from the stars and moon to work like they do on TV. During long nights on patrol, my finger perpetually twitched above the trigger guard, waiting for the moment when I could flex it, flip the safety mechanism, and travel to the trigger popping off rounds into shadows and dust. I would sit in the dark night after night, next to men, but utterly alone in the blackness. I knew *they* could be anywhere. They were shadows.

It is often easier to confront a fear you know is there rather than an imagined worry. In the hundreds of patrols over my two tours, the most fear that I saw was in the unknowable, in the shadows. Constant vigilance was our motto, but worry was my plague.

April, Second Battalion Seventh Marines disappeared into Marine history in support of Operation Vigilant Resolve (The First Battle of Fallujah). Our objectives revolved around capturing towns and strongholds of suspected insurgent activity along with the Euphrates and into the Zaidon region a few dozen clicks south of Fallujah. We spent a little less than a week or two in movement capturing weapons caches and detaining military-age males who looked like they were up to shenanigans.

One night in late April, Golf Company made its way to the outskirts of a large compound called Ferris town. This town was a block, literally, a perfect square of government housing in high rises and derelict concrete shapes. In the middle was a water tower that looked out at all of the surrounding blocks with an amazing unimpeded view.

We dug in next to some artillery unit and scratched two-man foxholes in the hard ground before collapsing into them for a few hours exhausted coma. Early in the morning we were told what was waiting for us. As we mounted up into our armored troop carriers and popped open the roof hatches allowing us to stand on the seats and look outward, weapons at the ready, word came that this was a stronghold of former Baathists and Fedayeen. Again, the nerves of what I was about to do and see prickled through my whole body. As my tingling fingers checked magazines, and numbly shoved a forty-millimeter grenade into the launcher under the barrel of my rifle words of encouragement, threat, and curse drifted up from the belly of the armored beast. We would move into the compound in a column and blast away at any threat presented. We had mortars on call with pre-registered targets, artillery counter-fire batteries were waiting with thick steel shells excited to scream over our heads and find a target, or forty. The morning before, we drove by the artillery and they were arrayed impressively in line. There must have been a dozen big guns perfectly ordered, crews milling about, ammunition stacked up.

Helicopters were on call and overhead was the horrifically devastating Lockheed Martin AC-130 gunship. This was essentially the same plane that became famous in Vietnam by being a flying fortress of firepower. It toted two twenty-millimeter Vulcan cannons made of six barrels which were capable of firing up to six-thousand rounds-per-minute. The bullet that comes out of the barrel is thicker than your thumb and roughly the same length. When the round hits a soft target, or even comes near enough one, the object is not simply penetrated, but utterly eviscerated, whole limbs vaporize, torsos become pink mist and the human target simply ceases to be. Along with the mini-gun (seems to be a bit of a misnomer), there was usually a forty-millimeter Bofors cannon that fired high explosive rounds. If the Vulcan cannon didn't get you, the Bofors would. On top of this, there usually was a one-hundred and five-millimeter M-102 howitzer. When fired, the cannon actually moved the aircraft sideways in the sky. The frightening arsenal we had around, above, and with us that morning brought just a bit of comfort. Even with all the firepower, it wouldn't take much, just some unknown enemy to pop out from some rooftop with one lucky AK-47 round to take me in the neck, head, or any other part of my body I found vital to end me before the artillery, mortars, helos or Specter could help.

My vehicle was third in convoy into the city. The city was walled in the manner of a Moorish outpost. No wonder why we failed to make a good impression on the majority of the Iraqi populace when our understanding of life was so far from theirs. We looked to the roofs and our weapons followed our eyes up and around onto the balconies and rooftops. My finger hovered over the secondary trigger on my weapon that was attached to the grenade launcher under the barrel of my M-16. I was more on edge on the outskirts of Fallujah in a little compound than I have ever been in any other place and time.

We saw none of it. We were immediately hit by large volumes of fire of a different kind. Waves and yelled greetings pounded us and ricocheted off the sides of our vehicles. Our weapons pointed all-round, bristling like a porcupine's quills.

There was no relief. Just happiness, kindness, flowers. I would have preferred weapons.

Nothing made us have that feeling of relief and closure. We still just wanted to have combat. We looked for something, anything, to take the edge off. I'd experienced my first combat not long before, and knew what it felt like, and desperately wanted none and more of it, but knew that there was only one thing that could relieve the tension we were feeling. I knew then and still do know that the only thing to do was to flush out the enemy somehow. We needed to change tactics and do what the Marines do best. It didn't take much to break the patience of the enemy who were most certainly hiding out in the compound somewhere.

We made a show of driving around the complex, stopping, letting the back ramps of our huge troop carriers crash onto the dusty asphalt roads with a ton or more force. From the blackness within, two dozen Marines ran out, weapons up, fingers on the trigger, knees bent on the run and looking for any target. It must have been an intimidating display of force and brazen hubris. After about a half-dozen rounds of this, we made our way out of the gates and back to fighting positions to wait for the night.

There are only a few distinct images and memories I remember from the night that followed our initial triumphal entry down the main road. These memories are more troublesome than most from that deployment.

We knew guns hunkered down behind most doors in this town. We knew also that many combatants from Fallujah had moved towards Ferris Town as psychological operation spent days before warning everyone we would kill any person with a gun in our way.

We set to preparing almost immediately, which meant cleaning our rifles, laying in our foxholes and eating MREs while we griped about what happened that day, or what didn't happen. We waited for night to come, and as we did, the outline of the city walls slowly grew into blurry indistinguishable patterns and shapes. There were no lights from the city that grew into a golden blur. All we heard was the mournful and haunting call to prayer. It went on and on in a long string of wails and beautiful reverberating vibratos that characterized all I loved of the Middle East. In my dreams, I often hear the wailings that filled the night on the outskirts of Ferris town. They lure me into false security where I wait for my dreamscape to erupt into fire and death.

The command ordered my squad to conduct patrols after midnight. Specifically, we were to avoid the main gate and get in without the knowledge of the townsfolk and begin a patrol through the streets. We trained to destroy the enemy with fire and movement. So, I am sure we alerted the whole of the Zaidon region and not just all the wandering eyes of Ferris Town after midnight.

As we patrolled through the streets, completely on edge, raising our weapons to our faces and sweeping every alleyway, window and dark street with both the muzzles of our weapons and the blinding beacons of our flashlights, all surprise out the window. We walked around the town for several hours, sticking to the walls like a slime mold.

The squad came to a large open park. On all sides loomed multi-story blank-faced buildings with dark windows and balconies in which I was convinced I could see dozens of men on their knees holding AK-47s and RPGs, waiting for us to rush into the open ground of the park.

There we stood, unsure of how to progress. Our breathing heightened, dark and nervous eyes darted from face to face.

We knew we were about to get into a fight. It was inevitable.

I could practically see faces and shades fill the upper shadows of the buildings. Our exfil location was on the opposite side of the park from where we now stood, and there really was only one way through, our path, blank landscape, open ground. We had fucked ourselves well and now were going to suffer. The big open space surrounded by tall buildings made us a sitting targets. In a double-file we began to move forward, weapons ready in our shoulders, heads on a swivel following the muzzle looking up and swinging around. Waiting. Adrenaline pulsed through my body, my nerves tingled. It was the fight or flight. As a Marine, there was one option, we were going to assault through, and fight.

The grass was knee-high and by this point was mostly weeds, the kinds of weeds that scratch and make noise only when one wants to be silent and stealthy. The weeds moved slow and deliberate to the soft wind. The heads of grass flexed, asking us to come in. The fingers moved slowly as one, faster and more desperate now, faster as the wind gusted. Our time was almost up.

In the middle of the park sat rusted and decrepit swings and a slide which long ago children enjoyed, shrieking and giggling as the oiled joints and chains sent the little urchins skyward. Now, the swings creaked softly as the wind pushed the seats forward and back in the way ghosts of the past haunt the places of the world where people should not be. The grass itched across the rust, hissing soft songs of warning, or welcome.

This was a nightmare world I could not escape from. We were crouching and moving. All that moved with us were the rusted and creaky swings, the tips of the grass awaiting the next soft push, and a grasp of tired and scarred fingers.

We kept dispersion and slowly moved, making it halfway with nothing happening. At perhaps three-quarters of the way through, my mind exploded.

Nothing.

At last I came from a crouch and followed the man in front of me into a sprint to the safety of shadow and cover.

Nothing happened.

A whole squad of Marines broke a cardinal rule of patrolling and small unit tactics, with nothing worse than frayed nerves and chattering teeth.

We left the compound and with a collective sigh of

relief moved back to the hasty foxholes and slowly one by one drifted off into sleep. Still, not a sound, no talking, no hushed whispers, no fight. I really wish something had happened. I was still on edge, looking for a fix and finding nothing. I was still up there, and the adrenaline was still pounding.

Lying in my hole wanting, begging my adrenaline to come down and go back to normal did not help. I did not deserve the rush. I needed a fight, something to justify the worry. The tension kept up for days afterward. The string was taught and needed lessoning, but nothing would help. It is still wound up and needing to be released.

THERAPY

Things were not going well. Not in my mind at least.

"Paul, I think we have an opportunity here." We have been narrowing down the traumatic events for a main moment or event causing many of these stuck points. She stared directly at me pointedly and gave me the sense she was trying to flood my mind with theory, the thing I would need to know as well as how to help myself. I was oblivious. "It is clear as we go through your stuck points, as well as you talking. There are many places where you are retaining a traumatized state of mind." I wondered if she thought I was clinging on to the stuck points as comfort. In a way, I was. As we progressed through the therapy, I began to be more than a little resistant to the activities and homework. I didn't think about them during the week and would lie to her in therapy about my progress. I felt unique being wound up and hurt. It was how I had built an identity, my meaning and purpose was tied to my veteran identity, and I think I worried that would be going away with CBT. "I don't say that to imply that you are weak, but that the way you have internalized your situation and the events in the past, relating to the way you live in the present has been altered significantly." She droned on and I doodled while taking notes on her thoughts. I was changing my core beliefs and that can shake a man. We believed this idea that I got off lucky with my walk through the abandoned park that night years ago was one of the events sticking me down. "I have another event in mind that I think we will focus our attention on that you have alluded to, but we will continue to see what comes up. I was reading notes from your other meetings and remembering how you mentioned to me that you were asked by your prior therapist to make an exposure situation for yourself. Did you do that?" I nodded.

It was the spring of 2009. On a late-night walk with my then fiancé, we held hands and chatted softly about our future while walking through a suburb of Portland, OR and all was well. We would be married in a few months and all our conversations revolved around that future day in July. The scene in Ferris Town, half forgotten, sunk deeply in my mind, but then jarred awake. The walk was nice and carefree under the streetlights and stars until we turned the corner into an area that had four to five-story apartment buildings surrounding a common park.

There were only a few lights sending comfort down into the square. I immediately tensed up without realizing it. My heartbeat rose dramatically, and my breathing increased to a rapid short series of breaths. I had no idea what was happening. This was years after my last combat and even after the last hint of warfare crossed my path. Once more, I was back in Ferris Town. Once more the rustle of the grass in the breeze, the song of rusty chains holding swings, the lights on in the buildings, the few people on balconies smoking, drinking, chatting.

It was the closest I have ever had to a flashback; it was not even one of the times I fought.

I would not move into the square for some time until Abbie asked me what was wrong in that lighthearted way women ask men when nothing needs to be wrong. I was trying to mask my alarm, retie my shoes, find a reason to turn back. Nothing was wrong, but my reality had shifted just enough to convince me that the world was crashing in on itself. She coaxed me forward, but I moved slowly, eyes upward; I stayed in the shadows and watched. I envisioned the upper windows to be hiding shadows of rogue gunners and RPGs about to come through the curtains to blast Abbie and myself into dust, waiting for me to move into the open in order to turn me into pink mist and splattering viscera.

Abbie forced me to play with her on the swings and by degrees I became less and less worried by what I imagined. But the whole time my eyes were on the windows and roof, waiting for a perfectly coiffed head to pop up with a Lululemon headband on and a soviet grenade in her hand.

"So, the outcome was less desirable than expected?" She asked when I recounted the experience. I would say it was. I knew that putting myself willingly into the situation would be tough. After that night, I went back to my therapist in Portland and reported the feelings and emotions that were raised on my evening revisiting Ferris Town. She wanted me to repeat the event several more times, going back to the same place, during the same time, and during the daytime.

I never did. I was just too scared.

A VISIT TO
THE DEAD HOUSE
Road to Fallujah
April 2004

Glossary of Stuck Points #6: Unknown places harbor horrors. If I don't know a place, I do not know what could be lurking. Avoid!

When I was in infantry school, before joining my unit, I remember watching the HBO series "Band of Brothers." The 501st paratroopers led by Dick Winters liberate a Nazi concentration camp. For the men of the 501st, the fighting and near-constant warfare from Normandy to Bastogne to the Eagles Nest was suddenly justified in one discovery. Watching that particular episode for the first time on that day stays in my memory even a decade after the fact. In me, they gave voice to a brand of fear and misery I could never have dreamed up.

Shortly after this, I then began to hear all about the gassing and torture Saddam Hussein inflicted on his own people.

In infantry school, we were crowded into large auditoriums and shown videos of gassings, massacres, and Al Qaeda propaganda videos. This brought the "that sucks for them" thoughts that teenage boys have to an abrupt halt. I now know the intent was to let us all know what we were going to do, and why we were going to be fighting. I couldn't believe that in 2003, in our seemingly (at least to a seventeen-year-old) heightened state of morality we could have had our very own modern-day holocaust.

I was quite young during the Bosniac ethnic cleansing campaign in the nineties and it simply just wasn't on my radar. I think I remember it being another one of those short-sighted "glad I live in America" thought processes. Even in high school, no one really pushed any information out to us about it. I didn't even really know about American involvement during the fighting. I read *The Diary of a Young Girl* like all other 8th graders. We raise such foolish unworldly children here in America.

The mountains of Central Idaho were a great place to grow up if you like an older, crime and drug-free (relatively) area in which to spend your formative years, but not such a great place if you want to be aware of what was going on in the world. I mean, there was no cell phone service until 2003. Many people I know who live there until recently still lived under the oppression of dial-up internet and *Gasp* no 3G cell service. This is a place where one could not type up the BBC and make worldly and informed decisions. The Iraq war changed all of that for me.

Even still, there were only three enemies that obsessed many thoughts and coffee shop rants as if we really had any idea. Iraq/Afghanistan (actually, let's just expand that to the whole of the Islamic world according to some terrified folk), the reintroduction of wolves into Lemhi county and the Bitterroot Range, and those damn liberals. I really don't mean to stereotype whole swaths of people peacefully living in Montana, Idaho, and Washington, but after thirty years living in the rural parts of these states, this is simply my experience.

I remember Iraq's killing of the Kurds, the videos of gas attacks and the fact that we really did nothing. I am now generally against war, especially after quietly living with my own war for the last decade. It is really interesting that since the withdrawal of America from Iraq, and the resurgence of terror against those poor people persecuted by ISIS, my thoughts on war and American involvement are questioned and tested.

In 2003, when America invaded Iraq, a sense of justice came over me and I watched my high school class of sixty and their reactions. Back then I was all for war. I enlisted in the Marine Corps the year before on a delayed entry program and was headed for the infantry. That I was certain of. I wanted blood, I wanted war, I wanted some way to prove how manly I was. It didn't really matter who it was against. I look back at those years and the way I thought about things and laugh. Insert something here about the folly of youth I suppose. Well, I watched the news reports and followed the advance on maps like so many others had done following the landings at D-Day and Korea a generation prior. I really don't know where this crusading feeling came from besides youth. I was taught that insane fervor to a cause is very often a dangerous feeling.

I was ready to fight, but just needed to graduate high school first.

A year later in April 2004, we in Golf Company were well-traveled. In fact, we had traversed most of northern Anbar province in a matter of two months. I would hazard to say we were better traveled in their own country than most of the nationals we interacted with on a daily basis. But I guess that is not very fair since travel is not usually in the familial makeup of most Iraqi families. We were just returning to base after three weeks outside a town up north called Rawaa. These kind people were welcoming enough to give me my first fire-fight and my first few major IED blasts. As we returned, and quite literally before our socks dried out, we were given orders for a new offensive.

This was not just some patrol, it was not sitting at some checkpoint showing our middle fingers to drivers as they sped through the serpentine pointedly averting their eyes, and this was not even a company level operation. We were going to Fallujah, and this was a real offensive. There were battalions, there were artillery batteries, tank platoons, hunter-killer helo teams, Specter gunships. The battle plan was directed by General Mattis. General 'Mad-dog' Mattis was and is a cult figure in the Marine Corps infantry. He is a man's man, and one of the most respected battlefield generals in modern history.

He is noted for telling reporters that he loved fighting people, and telling tribal leaders that if they fuck with him, he would destroy them. More than that, he lived up to his promises, and he was generally feared by Iraqis and loved by his men.

Our mission was to be a sub-operation to Vigilant

Resolve, the first attempt to take Fallujah. Our role, called Operation Ripper Sweep, was to cut off fighters leaving the city from the north, and then as the Marines pushed into the city, move south and establish cordons to the west, and then to the south on a few towns suspected of hiding Fallujah's militants. The Rules of Engagement, those iron bindings that hold young Marines at bay were loosened so much so we were told to kill anyone wearing all black. I remember when being told this standing in a battalion briefing, I looked first to my squad leader and raised my eyebrows. Armas answered with a smile. I then looked to my fellow fire team member and roommate, Slavens. He and I met eyes and I think I saw a mix of excitement and worry. Slavens was the most capable tactician I knew, and even at that young age understood larger goals and side effects to our actions. I was still operating at a child-like level of tactical thinking. I think that in four years of the Marines I owe most of my knowledge of battlefield tactics and cause and effect warfare to him.

When we neared Fallujah, we were told we would meet up against company and platoon-sized elements of the "new Mujahedeen" waiting for us. I remember hearing about the Mujahedeen fighting the Russians in Afghanistan and hearing about how brutal and hard the fighting was. I was not particularly thrilled to hear this news, but it seemed the rest of the Battalion was as they were giving loud and en masse "oorah's" every few seconds and working themselves into a frenzy.

I wanted to kill. I wanted that first kill badly. I wanted to know how it felt to watch a body crumple as a double-tap of 5.56 thundered through them. I wanted to know what it would sound like, and what it would smell like, and what I would think and feel as I killed a man. A year later, when ramping up for another deployment, this time as the leaders, I wanted nothing more than to see no action and kill no men. How life changes so quickly.

This time, we found ambiguity, and it terrified me.

We lumbered south. As we slowly moved, we drove through palm groves and orchards, their dates and fruit growing thick and plump. I imagine 2004 was a good harvest for the Euphrates region of Al Anbar. Villages, some thriving, the residents coming out to wave, or stare, or in some cases show us the bottoms of their feet made for good viewing. We were tourists. We responded with waves, or middle fingers, or for those showing us their feet, we trained our rifles on them, making the rebellious children scamper back into their huts. In swaths the children came out, and surrounded us when we stopped for a security halt. They wanted candy, they wanted to learn English words like "Fuck off" and "I am the devil."

There are only three things about tracked vehicles.

1. The diesel fumes mixed with sweaty bodies make one perpetually nauseous

2. They are loud

3. They are not that bulletproof. In fact, they are bullet sponges.

If you are lucky, the top hatches will open, and you can stand on the seat and poke your head out of the hatch for a view and the ability to breathe without making your lungs flammable. They are loud all the time. I am talking like a hundred plus decibel level sustained for as long as you are in the vehicle. The crew gets these nice headsets, but the passengers are given nothing but headaches. Finally, you are cramped in a space no bigger than would normally hold ten people with twenty to thirty. And all the men are in full combat gear making them twice their normal widths. The armor of 2004 was not the same as it is now. The days of plate carriers had not yet come, and the old interceptor vests were heavy, awkward, and very non-breathable.

We drove for two days at twenty-five miles an hour stopping often for security halts. These consisted of the hatch dropping suddenly, and everyone piling out as if a rabid weasel were dropped through the hatch and started biting the men's dick tips. It was always frantic and the men ran out to catch a minute of air, stretch their legs, and take a piss, often while kneeling with their weapon pointed to some distant building. After some unknown time that could be five minutes, or three hours, a succession of yells would echo down the convoy, each sergeant bellowing the order to remount. The convoy continued. As time ticked by, the enthusiasm changed from one of elation and fear to discomfort and boredom. We were supposed to be slaying bodies already. And the only things that had been slain were MREs and some smell receptors courtesy of vomit, farts, and diesel.

On the second night, the command looked for a place that we could bivouac. They seemed generous in not wanting to make us dig foxholes for the night.

Foxholes suck to sleep in.

So, when we heard over the radio that they had found a building my platoon and another were going to peel off from the rest and sleep in, it was met with some relief. Buildings meant we could take off our armor and boots. As we drove up to our new home, my enthusiasm was heightened. It was a long building with a central housing of two stories with two wings off from one side and the other. The whole place was fairly windowless and austere. It was all thick concrete and had no markers or distinguishing plaques anywhere. It was just some random building sixty miles from anywhere, literally anywhere out in the desert. The well-worn dirt road ended at the front of the building and curved up the hill where we sat and scoped it out. It looked empty, and I overheard someone say it was not on any map...oh well, still better than a foxhole, I said.

Around the building were pipes, spools of razor wire, and concrete. Sandals and shoes were visible, scattered around, so the building hadn't always been empty like this. We drove down and unloaded all our vehicles. The gun team I was in, as well as a few others, began searching out and clearing the building. Weapons at the ready, I walked through the large central double doors followed by my team. We slowly moved into the left-hand wing to look around. A long central room, chipped and cracked concrete, and cinder blocks opened up holding in the black and heavy air. The floor was rough concrete, and central pillars rose to the ceiling every twenty feet down the length of the building. It was poorly lit and had a few single bulbs and halogen strip lights hanging from the ceiling. It was lit only by the fading light as it stole wherever it could through the small windows. The windows were man height and narrow, perhaps about two to three feet wide and inset into the concrete a foot deep. They appeared to be thick glass and beyond them was a walkway and beyond that, more razor wire and beyond that, the emptiness of the desert. Inside the building were rows and rows of showerheads. In this wing alone were perhaps one or two hundred showerheads. The ones I looked at were rusty and bare.

If they were to be turned on, would they release anything but long past screams that echo through the pipes? Was all of that in my imagination? Was this in fact a totally innocent place, or was my worry founded?

By now, other Marines moved into the building and began to fill it. Some groups moved sleeping bags and weapon systems into corners and staked out sleeping territory. Some began to look around and at each other with a nervous and knowing look. Eyebrows arching in the way that they do when something has dawned on us, but we refuse to believe it. It is more in the eyes than the brows. The twinkle goes out of the eyes and they become dark holes. Many of the eyes I looked at in that moment had already seen death and fear. The eyes were hardened to whatever secret knowledge came later. The secrets were knocking at our doors and I could see many of us refusing to let them in. Others opened the door a crack and were scared of what they saw.

Many men now huddled in corners and adopted the posture and mannerisms of those who know they are in a shitty situation and can't do anything about it. Their heads were down, voices low, and subdued. They would try to not disturb the spirits almost surely in this place. Their eyes darted down the dark of the corridor. The lights from small knots of men dotted the darkness down the length. The dark threatened to snuff out the lights, and as flashlights and headlamps turned off, the air engulfed them fully and they disappeared from the world entirely.

Others began wrestling. They closed themselves off entirely to the building and let it be something that was simply a roof over our heads. Two people found fluorescent light tubes and had a quick sword fight that ended in a pop and shower of glass dust. They laughed, coughing in the dust and began wrestling on the floor in the shards and dust. Some gathered around, laughing, heckling, encouraging punches and submission holds.

We woke early around five and began to leave. I cleaned my weapon and stowed my gear. A clump of men made a smoking circle and smoke drifted up like an iron smelter. I met with some friends in another squad and we climbed the hill to the track. We noticed two things. First, the tracks parked on top of a series of graves. The earth heaped in hummocks, and little markers trampled over by the tracks. Second, below us were a series of holes dug into the earth. They were dug out with a dozer and backhoe and hastily filled in again. There were perhaps five or six of them. The same feeling I'd had earlier that night came back to me.

Innuendo can do a lot to someone. Days later I would read about Marine units in Fallujah kicking in doors and going into basements only to find torture houses covered in blood and body parts. Memories of men and women brutally raped, mutilated, murdered, who'd spent countless hours begging for death. Many of those who did so never knew why they were being tortured. Many were mentally handicapped and only knew the pain they felt. And now I thought that many were dragged out of their houses and villages to die in a shower and firing squad within the walls of the dead house. I wracked my brain for some way to explain the presence of the building. I wanted it to be anything besides what it seemed.

The death tolls that are thrown about in conversation when folks back home discuss the Iraq war are sometimes staggeringly high. (Let me correct myself, I should have used the past tense; no one but Iraq war veterans ever discuss Iraq anymore, unless it deals with how much President Bush Jr. was an idiot, or what of a waste it was.) I have no doubt that the civilian toll was exceedingly high. I was a simple Lance Corporal and didn't know or care at the time but have a much better picture now. I know that no matter how high the civilian count was, it can't be as high as those killed by Saddam and his followers. The killing of civilians can never be forgiven. I imagine that is why we struggle so much with our involvement in the war. It started out as killing fellow soldiers but, in my time, turned to terrorizing the populace in many ways the same that Saddam did for years prior. When I consider what that house could have been, what I constantly land on was that it was a reminder how much the population of Iraq, many families having lived there several thousand years, would continue to struggle with what we provided them.

We left that morning, all ready to head out. We were ready to move to places that were not scarred with dirt and wards of showers. What we were moving to was a city of pain and torture houses. We were replacing a place of potential and suspected misery to move to a city where misery and hatred boiled over towards those who were not the same, those who did not trace their theological history to the same caliphate, to a place where inner religious hatred ran so deep that the 'others' were tortured, raped, brutalized and ultimately killed so their bodies could be dumped in the streets.

THERAPY

She stopped me before I made it to the place I called the death camp. I looked up from the ground and my memories to see she was a bit flustered. "So, Paul. I think I know where you are heading with this story, but I am going to be honest with you, I'm a bit hesitant to listen to the rest." She too remembered watching the reports of Kurd gassings, but had never really wanted to embrace it. "Before I continue with the remainder of your story," she told me, "We need to go over a few things first."

1. I needed to be thinking about how this experience has changed the way I view the world, and

2. Could I take those changes and find some good in them?

She counted them off on her fingers and held those fingers out for me to see. Her voice was insistent and her eyes a little wild, more so than her usual kind and distanced expression. I had hit something deep seated and fearful with this story.

"Telling stories makes no difference unless we can use them for some good or to purge the bad. This was no doubt a momentous occasion in your life," she said, and she was right. I could go down to the local VFW and tell stories; here, we need to work through them. That was a way that many of the older generations worked through grief. They told stories before therapy became even nominally mainstream and not taboo. "Tonight, on your drive home, I want you to think about how you can use this story."

I left the office that afternoon doing just that. I drove through Spokane, over its railroad tracks and deep into its historic residential center to my favorite place for a post therapy pint and sandwich. This was my therapy routine. Before driving home along the wheat fields of the Palouse stewing in whatever revelations or problems came up, I sat at a copper-covered bar top for an hour, drank a pint of Guinness and chatted with the bartenders over a ruben and corn pasta. Telling these stories in my head was something I was used to. I did it every day each time I walked, ran, showered, worked in my woodshop, ate, any time I had to myself. Admittedly, I was partially doing this to keep the memory alive, and partially because my mind wouldn't let me do otherwise. I drove home over the Palouse hills and let the memories come and wash over me. The wind washed over the stalks of winter wheat, snow collected along the burrows of the road and the wheat just memories themselves cut down to nubbins I drove and thought and cried and worried about what would come next if I were not able to get a handle on myself and my thoughts.

FIRST FIGHT
Northern Al Anbar Near Haditha
March 2004

I held onto my legs with one hand, trying to bring them through my chest. My knees—no matter how hard I pulled—could not get close enough. The other hand held my weapon, an M-16 with M-203— a forty-millimeter grenade launcher latched to the bottom of the barrel. I clenched the stock, turning my knuckles white as bleached bone. Somehow, by that intuition the soldier and warrior have had since swords were first forged, I knew if I let go of my weapon, I would die; it was more important than collapsing my chest cavity with my knees. I have found that in combat, what is important, ordinary, or even mundane would strike a normal person as simply insane. Nothing seemed more important than holding on to that rifle. It was my heart outside my body, hard, cold, and black. It waited impatiently to beat.

The bullets streaked overhead. They came innumerable; although if I tried counting, I think the legion of lead and iron was in the hundreds. Shooting stars, entering the atmosphere to careen towards, I thought, just my rock with reckless and unmitigated consistency. Dozens came shooting by. Some pounded the rock I hid behind into dust, sending shards of shattered limestone onto my helmet, bouncing playfully on my cheeks and neck. My short and hurried breath inhaled them with dust and other detritus, coating my mouth in a paste. More bullets whizzed past me, some so close the concussive wind blew harmlessly in a gentle breeze onto my face. These bounced off the cliff wall behind me to fall at my feet or ricochet in all directions. Luckily, they decided to avoid me once slamming into the wall.

Let's take a step back for a second. If we don't, then this story will be nothing more than just another combat masturbation, and there really isn't much room for that kind of story here.

For the Marine, and especially the Marine infantry-man, there is one achievement that is sought after more than most ribbons, badges, certifications and any other accouterments that may be given for some success in and out of the classroom. This is the Combat Action Ribbon, or for the army, the Combat Badge. It is something that sets aside the wearer as a person who has shared an experience with every warrior who has ever walked the dusty sands, frozen ground, or lush jungles of history. When a man or woman experiences warfare on the level that combat brings, no matter how short, long, or brutal, forever one walks in the footsteps of the heroes of antiquity. I do not say at all that we are put on the same pedestal of Achilles, Hector, Sgt. York, Chesty Puller, Gene Autry or any of the heroes we grew up with, but just that one shares a piece with what they all saw in their lives.

There is something interesting about those who have been in combat that really no one else obtains. Call it a new look, a new persona, a new feeling, whatever. Combat changes a person, we can see that. I remember hearing first how it changes someone when I read *All Quiet on the Western Front* as a kid in middle school. The pages spoke to me in a way I have never been able to let go. Remarque spends so much time up in the ether, in the phenomena of experience that we only come down to the battles of World War I as a byproduct of narrative. I remember reading it first sitting in the hallway outside Mr. Borne's 8th grade history class at lunch. I didn't pretend to know what was going on, but I knew something was different, that Paul, the protagonist, was different. He was a scholar thrust into war. Only when I was in my twenties and reading the book again did I realize what combat was to Paul. It was first a glory, then a badge, and finally a veil that kept him separated from others. I now teach this book to all my sophomores and spend extra time with those who revel in the scenes of battle and hand-to-hand combat.

I wanted to be mortared, I wanted to have Artillery scream over my head, and I wanted to fight an enemy. Perhaps because I was unpopular in those years and fed on stories from *The Iliad* and *Norse Myth* after reading *All Quiet*, I wanted to know for myself what it was all about, and most of all, I wanted to see what combat was, and how it changed people outside of a story.

We were heading far north one morning. We were leaving the safety of Baghdadi and Al Asad past Haditha, the Haditha Dam, and into Rawaa. It was spring in Al Anbar province, and after 0200 hours the wind would pick up into a howl, bite, and gnaw at us. It was the kind of wind that skipped flesh and muscle, and made one ache straight to the bone. We rolled out of the gates of Al Asad airbase at 0400. My squad leader, Corporal Armas, posted me in the LT's vehicle with the rest of the team, my muzzle drooped over the tailgate immediately. All I could focus on was how fucking miserable life was. For god's sake, war wasn't supposed to be this way. This kind of war, driving around and waiting to be bombed was inglorious, cold, dirty, and frankly inconvenient. This kind of war was muddled. How did we win without a clear enemy?

When a Marine or soldier mentions to you what a special kind of misery deployment is, very often, they know. Well, they know if they have spent time outside the wire of the big bases on combat patrols or driving the MSRs. They know if they have endured the oppressive sun without respite for days or weeks in the same clothes steadily falling to pieces, the cotton feeding off your body sweat, never taking off their boots except to take off and change socks. They know if they have experienced below zero wind chill at night and eighty degrees a few hours earlier with no warming layers in between the times so as not to have to take off their armor. If they have had to endure the constant threat of mortar and rocket attacks, IEDs and ambush, they know.

If they know, they have overcome many long hours and days without sleep, living in filth, pushing down the often deeply troubling privation and all the perversion that spawns from it, enduring food eaten only to stay alive, and fighting against the constant anxiety and anticipation of combat that could arrive at any moment, but usually doesn't.

In a way, we all wanted it this way. That's why we signed up.

We were Marines and thought ourselves tough sons of bitches who would thrive in combat. In fact, it was all of our first combat deployments, and idealism was somehow still there for some of us. There were some of us who begged for it, like Barbo, a bulky and dangerously quiet Jamaican who disappeared like a ghost whenever a job needed doing—I envied this trait. Barbo often patrolled with fixed bayonet and pointed the knifed edge like a spear at kids who passed us.

My fingers, already deficient in circulation, froze in the frigid wind. Slowly we moved north from Al Asad towards Rawaa in the north, and in the early morning light our eyes drooped to the ground running away below. Everything we did see was tinted with the green of night vision and tunnel vision. Our arms and legs slowly drawn up to keep movement possible, our gasmasks chafing the skin of our legs as they dug into thighs. We went through hours of uneventful movement, driving due north at fifty mph on the MSR. The whine of our overextended motor provided a hum and vibration, which hypnotized and lowered the eyes even more, making it impossible to stay on guard. Even if one had gotten twelve hours of sleep the day and night before, the moment one stepped foot on the Humvees and absorbed the vibrations, their eyes dropped. My head bobbed over and again while I tried to hide my sleepiness from everyone.

I opened my eyes just as it blew over us in a wave of time-shattering concussion, in time to see the road lift up and rend the concrete behind my vehicle, and just in front of the seven-ton taking up the middle of the convoy. The half-circle of the concussive wave expanded into space around us, making my chest compress and all the air escape my body for a single moment of time. We were all about fifty meters apart. The smoke engulfed the seven-ton and drowned out our yells of panic and groans of fear. All I could croak out over and over was "IED, IED!" and "Holy fuck that was big!" and sadly, it was only loud enough for me to hear. I guess it was more of an astonished whisper than anything else.

The seven-ton blew through the shrapnel-laced cloud like a green lumbering dragon charging through its own flame blast. My team leader, Cpl. Hoover, who sat next to me, yelled up to the driver, "Everyone is ok! Keep fucking going!" Of course, we did not really know everything was ok. I had my weapon up, scanning for triggermen on the sand dunes. We assumed all was ok, and as the vehicle bounded along, we had to guess until we moved out of any range of future attacks. Maybe that is not the whole truth. I really hoped all was ok. I begged for it in my mind, and I prayed for it to be the truth.

The radios blared; the Lieutenant held it in the crook of his neck and calmly asked for updates on the seven-ton. "Golf Four Alpha, this is Golf Four Actual, status update, over." Silence, He repeated the order over the radio, "Golf Four Alpha, this is Golf Four Actual, please provide status update, over." His voice cracked a little in the resending of the message. The truck kept driving fast and straight, so at least the driver was alive. He must have gotten confirmation because in the whine of the engine I saw him breathe deep and nod and respond to some update,

"Roger, good to go. We'll keep rolling. Let's meet up at the ICDC HQ as noted before. Out." He gave us the thumbs up, and we all breathed easily. I looked at Slavens, and we both knew how lucky they were. Our brothers were in that truck, and a second delay on the bomb and they would have all been killed.

We kept barreling onward and met with some of the Iraqi Civil Defense Corps soldiers—and I use the term very loosely (ICDC). They were pretty much all old Baathists and former Iraqi soldiers who glowered at us with dark eyes and still hated us, but were good at showing little open hatred. We thought them worthless fucks and wastes of oxygen. They were certainly not soldiers. Not like us. When we parked in line, all eyes were on the seven-ton. We all gathered around the truck and looked at the damage. Shards of metal the size and length of two fingers had embedded in the windshield and undercarriage. A ray of iron like a lightning bolt stuck out of the windshield and the side armor was peppered like a porcupine with jagged shards. Overall, it looked miraculous.

Shrapnel is the real killing power in a war. Bullets are nothing compared to the devastation shrapnel induces. A bullet enters and exits; there is usually one of them at a time, and the body armor prevents them from ripping through most vital organs. During my tours, very few men were killed with bullets. Shrapnel is often jagged without blunt edges. They are serrated knives of all shapes and sizes and fly in every direction in the tens of thousands (depending on the size of the explosive). They erupt outward and tumble, ripping and tearing through anything, enemy, friendly, children, women. No one is safe or spared from an IED, grenade, or mortar round. The superheated metal could find seams and nooks in the armor we wore.

Shrapnel has had many names over the years but earned its common and modern name from Major General Henry Shrapnel of the British Army. In 1784 he perfected (with his own means nonetheless) what he called spherical case. It was shot from a cannon over the heads of the enemy where a fuse would ignite the explosive in the case sending musket balls flying in all directions. If the fuse was cut correctly, the case would explode directly over or in front of the enemy, creating massive casualties and moreover demoralizing the enemy often to a point where it would simply stop fighting. This was one of the British's most closely guarded secret of the Napoleonic wars and caused incredible carnage on the French's tactic of massing columns of men in a snake of blue that flattened most of Europe's armies. Shrapnel is a household word, and I wonder what its creator would think if he saw the extent to which shrapnel as an object has become a maiming weapon in modern warfare.

Twice I saw what happened when a man took a shrapnel blast full force. This was the second. In the dark, when I saw him, my flashlight beam flitted over chunks of flesh and my foot crunched on a thumb. His chest, now a gaping mouth. Nothing was where it should have been. Pieces of him dripped down walls and doorways leaving a trail of blood, marking the door mantle so the angel would pass over. I was and still am entranced. My mental snapshot remembers me crouching over him, marveling at the anatomy on display.

Thinking back on the IED and the seven-ton truck, I

suspect that the 'new Mujahedeen' just buried the explosives too deep to allow for maximum damage. They tamped the explosive too well—explosives burst out in all directions, but with the most force moving in the path of least resistance. If they are too well or deeply packed, it is likely to just shoot out dirt and smoke with most of the shrapnel and power losing killing momentum.

Our patrol left the ICDC headquarters and kept on truckin' north. We were about halfway to Rawaa and now that the sun had risen and the desert played with the rays of light in wavering curtains of heat and shimmer like lines of beads hanging from a doorframe, I enjoyed the rest of the drive. I learned to love watching the villages we passed by, seeing the people hunched over hoes and rakes in the furrows of grain. It was a simple life I knew I would never have, the air shimmering diamonds and the sand a blanket only ending in new mud brick houses and women making the morning's bread in a palm fire, crouched down to blow on the embers, hands together, children running around after goats and sheep. The honesty and innocence of those moments has stuck with me as well as the combat and has become colored by nostalgia, tempering the worst.

We ground our way north to a split in the road where we separated the platoon into two forces to guard two areas of road, each of us dropping to one knee automatically. Our main objective was to guard both the road leading to the bridge and the bridge itself so a battalion of Marines could come in and take over Rawaa.

What was the point? Rawaa was a bad fuckin' place. I distinctly remember a month prior feeling righteous justice as our mortars fell and the tower toppled and the prayers stopped in a garbled beauty. I don't really feel that anymore.

The powers that be mandated that Rawaa was not allowed to be entered by any coalition forces unless they were at least a battalion strong. Think of it, one tiny town halting our progress. Us, the United States, the power of power, can you believe it? They brazenly attacked the U.S. Marines with impunity. I cannot but admire their tenacity and dedication.

The afternoon sun waned, and the cold came back. The entrance to the bridge fell away in a steep canyon, and as the three vehicles plodded toward the checkpoint, I looked up at old fighting positions. I was just waiting for fighters to pop their little heads up and waste us in a rainstorm of steel. Shit, they wouldn't even need to keep down. A few magazines and all would be over in a few seconds. Nothing happened. Nothing hit us but paranoia and silence.

A guard in beat-up and oversized fatigues came into sight, slouching forward from his guard post at the edge of the bridge. Rawaa to the north bristled with impenetrability like a medieval fortress. We approached the guard with mutual dislike and distrust. I was not posted to guard our perimeter, but to watch the radio, so while ignoring the radio as best I could, I watched as our LT and Sgt. started talking with the head ICDC guard by a brick hut they called a guard post. Within minutes, a Marine on the machinegun swivel attached to the seven-ton facing the river saw a smoke trail and shouted "Incoming!" in a cry that broke off as he jumped from the turret.

For some reason, one of our senior lance corporals was standing on top of the cab of the lead seven-ton. I assume he was 'schooling' one of our machine gunners on how to use the fifty caliber. (Senior Marines cannot help but show their "mastery" to their young wards, as if the young Marines had never seen a gun before.) The rocket oozed its way toward us. We all dove for cover. I jumped into the vehicle and slammed the door. The reporter ran into the brick outhouse attached to the hut. Billy jumped from the cab. He fell. The explosion came above us like a flak round in an expanding ball of black smoke. Billy was airborne and landed with a sickening crunch and moan.

Our platoon's first casualty, and it had to be comical. I mean, the guy jumped almost fifteen feet in a panic. How he didn't break anything still boggles my mind. Doc Avelez patched Billy up, and a dust-off called to medevac him. Billy wandered around our little area a bit dazed with full combat gear and no pants. A blue and bloody ass cheek was hanging out. Poor guy. He was shunted away from the bridge to our rear vehicle to wait for the helo and was placed onto a stretcher behind one of our vehicles. In the evening sky, the stars began to move and streak down. The sun was almost set, and in the coming darkness, the constellations shifted forever.

There were hundreds of them flashing high and lightning-fast through the atmosphere. Someone yelled to take cover again. I looked around; there was the guard post, two armored vehicles, and the seven-ton. Marines scrambled for them. Where should I go? A rock the size of a small trashcan lay about ten feet from the side of the cliff, and despite all my training and common sense, I dove for the rock.

As the stars walked down the sky to illuminate us, I cowered and curled my legs into my chest. It couldn't have lasted more than thirty seconds, but in those thirty seconds, my life moved at a vastly accelerated pace behind that rock. I grew old and died over and over again. I traveled in time and let eons pass as the seconds slowly ticked by. I'm sure I whimpered and cried out, maybe I screamed in the whizzing and zipping of rounds. This was my first direct combat, and it was nothing like I pictured it in my head.

Fuck John Wayne and the Dirty Dozen.

There was nothing glorious in this kind of combat, cowering behind a stone while the bullets pinged off the vehicle armor and zipped past my ears, cracking into rock and steel. Billy was screaming in what I assumed was both panic and pain; protecting him, two other Marines were doubled over, laughing hysterically pointing between me and Billy. All I could do was crush my chest with my knees, watch Billy moan and scream, and try to force myself back.

As the dust from the first bullets still rained down, it all ended, and I lay there not knowing it was done until Gunny Dobbins boomed in a deep voice barely audible over the cacophony of silence to return fire. Behind me, another sound razed the foundational silence. The slide of an M-240 machine gun racked back with a monstrous movement of metal against metal, slamming forward and being thrown backward with a force that probably drew sparks. And the fast heartbeat of our bullets started pumping blood and fire—the pent up anxiety from months of nothing—over the river into the village that just tried to annihilate us. The flame from the barrel of the M-240 erupted two feet outward like the breath of a dragon. I jumped up, raised my rifle, and flicked my finger without thinking. I yelled, I screamed, I lost myself in the violence of action that was pent up in me. I dumped round after round into the town. Indiscriminately shooting at any building downrange. I lost all discipline and just shot until the empty magazine forced the weapon's action to lock, ready for a new magazine.

The fight ended as it started, in silence and enveloping darkness. The last of the tracer rounds disappeared into the walls and alleyways of the village, and the heavy and quick rhythmic breathing of two dozen bodies became audible as lungs echoed the burps of the machine gun. No movement, then all at once, the spell was broken.

Corporals and sergeants barked orders, "Slavens, get that gun up! Reload your weapons! I need an AT-4 on that hillside! Let's fuckin' go gents! Gun teams started running up the hills, and the LT yelled at me to take a rocket up the hill overlooking the bridge east of our position. I grabbed an AT-4 rocket, a long fiberglass tube that held an explosive round eighty-three millimeters in diameter and, throwing the strap over my shoulder, ran across the road and down a trench before the hill began.

Our ICDC bridge guards, all weapons forgotten, huddled in a ditch and cowered. Some of them were crying into their hands. Some prayed. Seeing them, I raised my rifle instinctively at the first I saw and without thinking, clicked the weapon off safe. My finger hovered and twitched slightly. I really wanted him to be my first kill. I ached for it. My adrenaline controlled my body, and my mind struggled to keep up. It flicked through my mind that these cowards didn't deserve to live. The fuckers probably called in our position and timing to their friends in the town. My mind caught up, and I flicked the safety back as one stood up below me, indignant that I would point my weapon at him. I yelled and raged at him. I wanted to put a round into his eyes. I wanted them all to die and remember wondering if I could get away with it by saying they drew weapons on me. I could've chalked up half a dozen kills.

They ran.

As one, they bolted to our rear. Letting them go, I ran up the hill to a good overlook position in front and to the east of our new machine gun emplacement. There was a large killing field in front of me where the bridge stretched out into a few hundred meters. I was to destroy any vehicle that tried to break through our lines, probably with a VBIED. I primed the weapon, opened the sights, put my fingers on the pins, ready to pull them out and flick the trigger. I knelt on one knee, my elbow resting on the other. I measured the distance and thought about car speeds. How much would I have to lead the vehicle? Should I aim way ahead of it and blow a hole in the bridge on the off-chance that he couldn't swerve? What if I didn't lead well enough and he made it through to hit our men? Would that be all my fault?

What happened next?

No vehicles sped over the bridge for me to blast, no more shots were fired. Nothing. The adrenaline still pumped in my blood, numbing the nerves, and the next hour went by in a blink. We pulled our men into the vehicles, and I dumped my rocket onto the floor

We threw our trash from the day out the back of the truck and frantically drove back to the rest of the platoon a few miles away. Just away from the post, the vehicle in front drove on, suddenly engulfed in black smoke that I could barely see in the dark as an IED exploded around ten- to fifteen-feet off the road peppering the truck with iron. Exhausted from the adrenaline wearing off, we all drifted off to sleep on the quick ride, and no one noticed that our vehicle was hit by another IED. The adrenaline that pumped through us ebbed away and left us dead to the world. When we woke up moments later, a large ribbon of the vehicle's bed was torn away as a piece six inches long ripped through our vehicle, hovering just over the floor of the bed embedding itself into the kevlar floor cover.

Recently, I met up with my old squad leader, Armas, after sixteen years of not meeting at all. We got drunk and chatted with his wife listening as we both spouted stories and asked questions of each other about gaps in our memories. "Dude, I thought you all died that night." Armas said as he told me what he felt and saw as he drove us away from Rawaa. "You were all asleep and when the truck got rocked by the blast, I looked back and you were all slumped over. Shit, I was convinced I was the only one alive in our truck." I stared. I remembered Armas slapping us on the chest when we stopped and looking at us with a little more love and care than usual. This news rocked my understanding of the narrative of these stories. I had thought all these years that it was a small blast and all was well, but he was telling me a totally different twist to the story.

"We slept through a direct blast?" I couldn't believe it at first but remembering the rips in the floor of the vehicle, it sounded true.

"Fuck yeah. I was convinced I was the only one left and

just at the blast, my arm on the radio went numb. We were driving blacked out, so I couldn't check anything out. My arm went numb, and I felt a warm dripping down my side. I drove frantically the whole way, convinced I lost my arm and you were dead." I just stared at him over my wine glass and tried to comprehend what was now the story. "Yeah man, it fucked me up for a long time. I made peace with it all on that drive."

We met up with the rest of the platoon who had secured the crossroads. Whittington, a machine gunner, and I were placed on a rooftop to watch the desert to the west for the next eight hours. We spent the hours both coming down from adrenaline, and almost unable to keep our eyes open. We took turns. Fifteen to thirty minutes on watch while the other curled up in a bivy sack and rested in a stairwell, protected from the wind and cold. It was a blur of misery. The winter wind whipped up sand on its way to us and stung my face. Even when not on watch, I stayed awake most of the night. When on watch, I still expected to see men poke their heads over the sand berm and engage us with rockets and small arms. Nothing happened, yet again. Along the road, a battalion of men in vehicles slowly plodded on in columns like the Macedonians who made their way through two-thousand years prior under Alexander.

The night ended slowly, and my eyes refused to stay open. The sun crested the desert and made the silica sparkle like half-buried diamonds. We made our way back to base, several hours drive away, uneventfully and in a haze. I remember none of it until we were back, unloading explosives and ammo. I helped Slavens and Whittington unload thousands of rounds of ammo and heavy machine guns and hump them back to our room. Once back, we all gathered as a platoon, and our lieutenant and platoon sergeant looked at us, and their eyes told stories of pride and expectation that words failed.

We were men. I was eighteen years old, and not even a year before had been a boy in high school. We were men.

SURVIVOR'S GUILT
Spokane, Washington 2012

Does the feeling of guilt over not sharing in the same terrible fate of your brothers' change who one is at the core?

As I have spent time driving to therapy over the years, I have devoted probably too much time alone in my car thinking about what it means to be a survivor, and how it really can change someone.

What really is survivor's guilt? As a human, many of us feel guilty often for our actions, thoughts, and words with regards to our other members of humanity. I feel confident I can assert that fact. Guilt makes us go over a variety of reactions. Guilt is an immensely powerful emotion; I would say one of the most powerful in the spectrum.

Survivor's guilt is one of those weird anomalies in the human psyche that so often comes and goes with such little attention attached to it, and with so little understanding at the time of the manifestation. It was interesting to view the response Marines had to these attacks we experienced in 2005. We knew the main

183

combat in Fallujah and Ramadi was far from over. It would take another two years for that to happen when in 'the surge' the Marines, helped and led by my unit, trampled the rest of the resistance to the coalition forces. What was interesting to see and feel in my body and mind was the blood lust that would come in the aftermath. When in Iraq, we had to act as peacekeepers and law enforcers. We were nation builders, as ironic as that was. It was as if you put deranged psychopaths in charge of a water treatment plant and gave them cyanide and told them to keep an eye on things, perform maintenance and do not touch the cyanide. What the fuck did they think was going to happen? The Marines began to do what they do best; when losing many of their friends to IED blasts and trigger-happy snipers, anyone and everyone is an enemy. The rule to 'look at everyone one as if they are an enemy' was just difficult then to not treat them all as if they were.

One incident in particular stays in my mind. Towards the middle of my last deployment in 2005, before we picked up and moved into the countryside, my squad was on a routine patrol through a neighborhood that lay to the south of Main Supply Route Elizabeth moving west to east and to the west of ASR Henry which bisected the city running north to south. This was below an area we dubbed the "pizza slice." Geographically this was from the intersecting roads that cut a section of the city, their graveyard, into a rough-looking pizza slice. On this one patrol, our Lieutenant came with us, and we stopped off at a house. We heard there was one man living there in particular that was very good at making bombs. We knocked on the gate with the heel of our boots and didn't wait to ask permission as the door flew back on its hinges from the blow. The squad poured into the courtyard, weapons trained, the man behind covering the front and quickly, in a practiced and efficient manner, entered and cleared the house, detaining the owner before he even knew what was happening. As he wasn't hostile at the time and was searched, we left his hands free for the moment so we could bring in an interpreter and talk to him in a more relaxed and trusting atmosphere. He didn't want to honor the trust we placed on him, and lashed out at the lieutenant, a short man whose soft-spoken voice betrayed an intelligent demeanor and a fairly judicious sense of fairness stuck in a small body. I was the platoon and squad radio operator and followed this man like a much taller and ganglier shadow. I rarely left his side, and we watched out for each other on patrols. I was not paying close enough attention.

We should have shot him on the spot. We were in all rights allowed to do so. A known enemy tried to attack our officer with the intent to take his weapon, but before anyone could put anything into his chest, the lieutenant hit him hard and he dropped fast. This is where his worldly problems started, because we had been itching to take some measure of revenge on anyone for losing five of our friends and were largely unencumbered with the moral scruples that would have stopped us from making a man suffer for what his countrymen did earlier to us.

We secured his hands tightly behind his back with Flexi-cuffs and dragged him to the Humvee, throwing him in the back. He lay there, on the soft kevlar covering bleeding and making a small mewing sound. He looked pathetic. He was thin and dark with a short beard I suspected was just coming in for the first time. His facial features, though mostly covered by a blacked-out pair of goggles poked out like knives. His chin and cheekbones, sharp and defined, clenched with what was about to happen. No one wanted to be detained by Marines in Fallujah. We were wolves. We were starving, sick, and vengeful.

In my post-military life, I often think about this and wonder if I should be ashamed. I go back and forth according to my mood, but I am usually not ashamed. Sometimes in order to fight brutal guerilla warfare, a higher brutality is needed. We wanted to be feared, not respected. We wanted to have them all know that when you fuck with Marines, only prolonged pain comes out of it. We were not nation builders, we were warriors.

I walked into the vehicle, shut the Iron Gate behind me with a heavy clang. This was a broken shell of a man that hadn't seen a fraction of the pain he was about to endure. My rage spent itself in pity as I looked down at him.

We loaded into the vehicle and I took my seat in the front with the air conditioning and the radio. As we moved down the street, I heard snippets of what was happening in the back of the vehicle, and only found out later the man who attacked our lieutenant needed a medic.

We made it back to base and threw the man, still cuffed, into the shipping container that served as our detention facility to await the corpsman who was going to assess his state, and then the HET (Human-intelligence Exploitation Team) Marine. They were psychologically brutal and physically rough. These were guys who locked the door on the way in to a room. No visitors. No witnesses. Only results, but if they could extract info that would save our lives, and the lives of our men, we were not about to complain or raise red flags.

War is not about kindness. War is about staying alive. Whatever it takes.

I knew this from my first deployment, and it rang true still. The corpsman came and reported that the man should go to the hospital. He would go to the hospital only after HET talked with him. This man was left alone in the connex box and was no longer our problem.

I wonder what his name was. I wonder what his story was.

There have been so many questions in the years since then that complicate the narrative in a way I am uncomfortable with. I should have been uncomfortable then. Our thirst for action was slaked, and for myself, as I sat on the balcony of our platoon living area letting the breeze start to dry my salt-caked uniform, I closed my eyes and wondered what I had just done, or if I had begun to repay a debt I owed to the five whom I should have been amongst, the five like Gunny Dobbins who was back in the states having surgery performed on his neck and arm.

I began, much like I do almost daily now, to remember the names of those I knew from infantry school and my unit who had died since we had seen each other last, and as the number of faces in my mind mounted, I just wondered more. Would I ever repay the debt I owed them for not falling with them? They fell, they were blown to pieces or shot, or lost in the world of pain and suffering until they put a gun to their head and actually pulled the trigger. Could I ever remove the feeling that I should have been there and possibly taken someone's place? I knew that if given more opportunities to pay back the enemy for what they had done to others, to my brothers, I would without hesitation. The hesitation comes later. We already had too many purple hearts in my unit, and if I could avoid more by instilling fear in people, I would. This was a matter of staying alive and saving my brothers. After all, it's about the guy next to you, and that is the whole of the world.

<u>Glossary of Stuck Points #7</u>: Because I abused others, even by my refusal to speak up, and acted in an immoral way, I am an immoral person, and must pay some kind of penance.

THERAPY

It is easy to understand that things are going to take a while to become evident when they begin to change, but knowing the change is going to happen, and being patient for the change are two very different matters entirely. "Hello again, Paul. I am glad you made it today. I know that the weather has not really been cooperating with us, so I'm glad you made the drive." She said this while staring into my face fiercely, a kind smile breaking the intensity in her eyes. A few months into the program, the therapist suggested things were not getting any easier. The revelations and existential angst kept me up at night, but it also kept me reading. I began reading Kierkegaard and Sartre, Husserl and Marcel. I could label what was going on as an understanding of purpose and meaning, an attempt to live my life in an authentic manner. I had a friend, rather than the therapist, teach me the philosophy behind phenomena and meaning, and somehow it made more sense. Over glasses of wine at a restaurant he managed, the waiter/professor talked to me about what it meant to live authentically, and how to change our approach to life so we could do such. The necessity to understand had never been stronger.

Through the weeks of sessions, I became a master of my emotional responses and triggers. That is, when I remembered to be. Not only was it easier to recognize them in myself, but as I talked it became easier to identify where things came from. It was hard to believe this was actually working if only to make myself more aware of the differing ways to solve the problem I created in my daily life. It became easier to pinpoint individual nightmares. I knew for example, that when I dreamed about dripping blood or missing people, I could look back while using my new dream journal and find a connection to the IED in 2005. So, when I thought about the IED in 2005, I could understand a bit more about what it did to me at the moment.

The therapist gave me homework upon homework. I took a dozen worksheets with me each week. The instructions told me to write down feelings and emotions related to interactions throughout the day. Then I was supposed to analyze better reactions to those emotions which often drove me to undesirable behavior. One day's interaction sounded something like this:

"So, Paul, how have your homework sheets been helping you?"

"Well, in all honesty I forget to do them. Often something happens and instead of sitting down with a pen and paper; I go on with life and utterly forget to do them. Most of the sheets I have this week were written down later in the day." She went silent and stared at the ground.

"If you do not help yourself, Paul, I am not sure this is the right method. Are you sure you are interested in the stringent nature of behavioral modification therapy?" I was not sure if I wanted to continue either. We were a bit more than halfway through the twelve weeks but I was frustrated in not seeing much change. I was frustrated in her chiding remarks and the looks on her face when I didn't do my homework. I was frustrated at my memories that intruded on my sleep now that I was trying to think about them more. I was angry with myself for not being able to make the changes on my own from nothing but force of will and personal strength. I was afraid of not making enough change and failing at my new mission.

"Today, I want to take a different direction. I want to have you focus not on what gives you problems, or makes you nervous, but what makes you proud. We are going to take a small detour for a few minutes, and I want you to focus on your proudest moment since you, as you put it, 'started your new life.'"

It didn't start at boot camp graduation with my parents and grandparents watching. It wasn't being in combat and making it out alive or understanding some existential and definitive proof as to why I was fighting in Iraq. My proudest moment up until then hit me when I walked out of an airport bathroom.

I was in the Portland airport mid-2004, just finishing putting on my uniform for my family and well-wishers to see after my first deployment. The day was already a winner. I had been moved to first-class and had a double gin-and-tonic on the house...er, on the plane I guess, even though I had barely turned nineteen. "You're old enough to die for us, you're old enough to drink." She was a nice flight attendant—quite attractive too (a little blond with a button nose, a strong jaw and huge almond and green eyes, in case you are wondering). After we landed and disembarked, I took my uniform bag and went to the nearest bathroom to change. I was then thanked by exactly seven men who were in various stages of taking care of their business (one word of thanks even came out from behind a stall door...I didn't investigate).

As I left the bathroom doorway, I chose that exact moment to check myself and zip up my fly, and looking up, I was greeted by no less than fifty clapping travelers (good thing I had at least remembered to zip my fly). I shook men's, women's, and children's hands until mine were sore, and got hugs from many gorgeous women (didn't get any numbers though; the uniform only takes one so far). All this in Portland, Oregon of all places, the place I expected to be called names and berated for being part of "Bush's great rolling war machine." Nope, not a single mention, just lots of 'thank yous' and hugs.

Of course, the therapist was smiling. So, what did I learn from that?—definitely that one doesn't need to support the war to support the troops. They were clearly supportive, though many of them had peace buttons and some told me they didn't support the war but were proud of me.—what else do you take away from all this?—well, now I guess we have something over those Vietnam vets. Many of our problems don't come from being spit on or berated other public abuse. I think we can cross that one off my trigger list. In fact, I wonder if just the action of public thanks and recognition is enough to stop a trigger.— well, maybe there was more to be ashamed of back then. There were some terrible atrocities committed by both civilians back home, and soldiers.—no, I'm sorry, all wars have atrocities. All are equally abhorrent. All wars are atrocities but have become a necessary act by people. We are an odd race.

PHOTOS ARE ALL
I HAVE LEFT
Kalispell, MT
2005

I have this picture. My mother gave it to me.

The faded greyscale features my grandfather, Walt. He is leaning against a slightly rusted corrugated tin Quonset hut in Korea. I think it is rusting but the sepia tones make it exceedingly hard to decipher. He is smiling. The smile is thin and genuine, the kind I rarely saw cross his thin lips when I knew him. I met Walt exactly thirty-two years and five months after the photo was taken. Of course, I don't remember the first meeting of him, but seeing photos of me when I was days old cradled in his thin arms, the person I am now studies his smile in the same sepia tones. The smile is older and still genuine but torn by what I now know are memories that refuse to leave him.

I have another one of myself where I am smiling as well. I was on a combat tour like he had once been. The similarities are eerie. I stood in a doorway sometime in 2005. I was halfway through my second tour, and I stood naked but for a pair of silky running shorts, stained and ratty. They were my only pair left. I usually patrolled commando but I was on base in this photo in a doorway holding a coffee cup and smiling in the same way as Walt.

The *police action* that took place in the early '50s has some kind of an illicit mystery to it. It's a topic at odds to the smile on the young man's face and the posture. This is an almost tourist posture.

I find myself looking over my shoulder writing this. Looking for ghosts in the black doorways beyond me, beyond the photo, watching me break their generation and a half long maxim of pitying silence. The forgotten war was only forgotten by some. All wars are remembered by those who were there. It afflicted a generation, all understanding what it meant to suffer. The only suffering happening in our photos perhaps is that taking place in the two-tone black in the open door and the world beyond the edges of the paper. My mother always wondered how he suffered, I think. She would ask rhetorical questions to my dad, as if he would know, and they would chalk it up to a generalization of "The War" or something else having to do with his alcoholism or his introversion, or something else quirky or 'strange' about Walt. They couldn't know his pain, not due to some failing of their own, but due to the lack of experience in matters of war.

My parent's understanding of the Korean War for many years consisted of episodes of *M*A*S*H**. How could they know what went on in his head? Alan Alda does a good job of asking the tough questions of war veterans, but without the context built into personal experience, one could only speculate. It's ok. They don't need to know. Thankfully, that experience isn't known by all.

March 1953; the armistice that stopped the war was still 'on the way' after three years of horrible war (I think we can call it war instead of a police action since over 50,000 men died. If there is some threshold that needs to be passed, it was passed. The name "Korean Conflict" is a misnomer and insult to both sides of men and women who fought). The generals somehow could not, and still cannot, decide how to end the war. I assume our young Walt in the photo had some good ideas on a peaceful end of the war, as do most soldiers in all wars. It's interesting how young soldiers understand why we need to end the war, even if they couldn't jump through the hoops to get it done. It's worthwhile to listen to the young who are fed up with war rather than the old who no longer have to go themselves. But what do I know?

There is a scene in our reoccurring novel, *All Quiet on the Western Front*, where our main character, Paul is with his friends after days in the trenches. They are joking about how to end the war and why war began in the first place. One of the men, Albert, one of Paul's classmates in earlier days, says, "...whether there would have been a war at all if the Kaiser had said no." To which Paul replies, "He was against it from the first." This is interesting since the solders didn't know the Kaiser instigated the war in that sense via the Schlieffen plan in an attempt to roll up France. Albert continues, "'Well, if not him alone, then perhaps if twenty or thirty people in the world had said no.'

'That's probable', I agree, 'but they damn well said yes.'

'It's queer, when one things about it,' goes on Albert,

'we are here protecting our fatherland. And the French are over there to protect their fatherland. Now, who's in the right?'"

Who is in the right? Who could possibly be in the right when instigating or retaliating? Whenever I teach this novel, I highlight this section with my students and ask that question. There is always a reason to fight if you think little and listen hard, communism, terrorism, the potential for future conflicts, but we must be cautious of who is calling for it, the old who won't fight, or the young who must die?

If I am to believe the long and loopy writing on the back of the photo, it was taken shortly before the end of the war. The forgotten script (I think the historians call it, "cursive"), a perfection of handwriting reads: *Believe it or not/ but this is me/ Taken at the RTO, Young Dung Po/ Korea, March 1953.* Looking it up, I see a *Yeongdeungpo* which is a district in Seoul. It looks like Walt is on a break from the war in the photo. The smile tells of someone on borrowed time who doesn't worry about what will come next.

Years later when he was an old man and shortly before his death, I would look through a tin of memorabilia from these years and come across what I imagine were in his pockets when the photo was taken. That is an exciting thought. It doesn't really matter in reality if the items were in his pockets. I want them to be, and since he has passed, I can make that choice. A pack of cigarette tobacco, still full with the wrapper still covering the contents, a receipt for the repair of a gold watch in some Seoul shop or another, a pipe in walnut burl, a compass, and various other things I can't remember. Walt was watching the news and didn't look over as I rummaged through his things of a past life.

When he was within a year of his death, sometime in 2015, I think, I visited his assisted living home in Colorado Springs and my Grandma showed me the tin. Inside was another photo from the same time. He was with a friend and a few girls. The men stood akimbo and the girls sat legs together, smiles on both their faces. There was a receipt for a watch repair in Japan. He paid four dollars for the work.

I like to imagine him walking into a shop late one night in Tokyo when he was recuperating from one of his many wounds. He would have been in uniform and perhaps running errands with friends, a brown paper parcel tucked under one arm. He would have told the proprietor that he was on limited time and was going back to the front in a few days. He just needed the work done so his watch could work again. An old man, perhaps, would have looked up at him and reassured him with nods and smiles that it would be done on time. Come back tomorrow he would have said in broken English. Pay now, come back later. Walt was young; he would have paid then and come back later.

I am conversing with the past and a young man I never knew and simultaneously an old man I did.

It's almost like looking into a mirror. I have heard most of my life that I look like Walt, tall, slender, big hawkish nose, sad eyes, though only now do I see it myself. He has always been a real enigma. A grumpy old man with a hint of the same smile. He seemed to always be caught somewhere between love and loss, the past and the present. The toothy smile he bared so readily hides much semblance of fear and loss though. The black and white reach forward through time and predict my own future, not too long ago when I too would become a lost man just like him.

I never really saw any similarity with Walt as a kid. When I would look up at him in his later years, his face was often partially impeded with a can of Lucky Lager, a brew I have often tried to find but seldom can. I really just want one can. I want to crack it and find if I can recapture some of the Walt I never knew. I want to crack it and see the swooping black hair under the cap, pulled back jauntily and the powerful frame hidden by green winter dungarees that look like they could not stop a Korean snowstorm. I want to be there. To become annoyed at the orderlies and privates who keep moving in front of the camera (as people not relaxing are apt to do). *Goddamnit all, we're trying to take a picture! Just one more try, Walt.*

I love his stance. He leans against the hut and projects a 'devil may care' haughtiness. That may be because I never really saw him relax in my own life, but the stance relays a certain enjoyment in the present. It's something we do when we are at home with family, a beer in hand, a carefree understanding of the world. This is not something we do in war, yet we both have photos that show it.

The hand thrust into his pockets regardless of regulations. Actually, I would like to think it was an open and flagrant middle finger at regulations. Here, I see more than a man. Walt was an old veteran. A veteran in the true meaning of the word. Almost three years in a war against ideals. A war that destroyed over fifty-thousand and propelled men and places to everlasting infamy. Porkchop Hill, Chosin, Pusan Perimeter. The smile gives little hint to the battles. Thanks to *M*A*S*H*, I can see beyond the photo, adding to my speculation. Here, I see a hint of irreverent Hawkeye. The stance just suggests he doesn't really give a damn if an officer walked by to rebuke him. The cover far back on his head; there is no pride in uniform. There is pride in being a man. No doubt about it, Walt is a beat-up old soldier.

The sign, thoughtfully cut off by some friend seems to say something similar to Replacement Battalion and the British RTO (or Radio Telephone Operations). Why he is in a British area, I have no idea. Perhaps the piano music floating through the air, giving free rides to good Tommy tunes. The gentlemanly air somehow pervaded even the rough and tumble enlisted club and drew Walt and his friends in. Were they about to enjoy a pint of something that should have been confiscated? I like to think Walt was supposed to go into the building and check out new gear for radio operators. Perhaps there was a new radio the British had, but in the end the beer sounded better than an afternoon with stuffy officers.

If this was a little rest and relaxation before going back up on the line, back on patrols, and back into death, it is easier to understand the lackadaisical smile. This would have been a night to remember. It was a time to take the new replacements to the e-club. (No doubt a corrugated tin building that did nothing to shield the cold March air. After all, wasn't that what the booze was for?) It was time to tell them how it really was on the line. It was a time to get them all to fear the enemy for all that happened to the men who occupied no space at all. *It is...well, you will find out how it is soon,* they would say as the wide-eyed replacements glanced at each other in turn, not wanting to lock eyes with these men who walked around with hands in their pockets and ratty perma-frozen uniforms. Walt and his brothers felt no joy in passing along the information but would do it nevertheless. They were new once too.

After the snapshot, Walt would most likely have repaid the favor. I wonder where the twin of this photo lies. Buried in some scrapbook, one that hasn't been opened but rarely since the attitude of the times told him to forget the war. The taker of my photo handing Walt the camera and quickly striking some pose of strength or nonchalance. The war would remain buried in photographs and memories and in the dreams that would burst forth from Walt the remainder of his life. Did his photo twin have the same problem? Did he also drown himself in booze in vain to forget all that happened? When his buddy went home, was he also told by family and officials to forget the last three years even happened?

Across miles and cultures, was there some North Korean or Chinese soldier laughing with his friends? With good music and a similar camera? Is it possible there would be another man, from another army leaning against the frame of a similar building, wondering when the war would end, and when he could go home to family? He too, would have friends who were lost, and a life shattered from a war only the generals seemed capable of justifying.

Walt would have been in his early twenties, and already those pixelated eyes yell a story largely lost. They have seen the semi-arctic wastes of the Chosin. They now speak of supreme privation. Patrols, ambushes, listening posts. They have changed since I last looked. Legions of Koreans and Chinese have all contributed to these eyes.

What camp was this? Was it close to the front? After

the photos were taken, was the camp rocked like it was so often with outgoing heavy mortar fire? The mortars, conveniently placed behind the replacement barracks thundered out their low and ground-shattering thump that meant infantry support, and like all old soldiers, Walt rarely flinched, but maybe swore once or twice at the power rocketing out to the hills all around. The smile, lingering just for a second more, realization that someone else was on the line this time.

What happened to what Walt saw, now so many years past? How many friends did he see blown up, shot? These eyes that look at us through the decades speak to the family of something more.

Who owned the camera? Did he make it out of Korea? Was he inseparable from Walt? Is that where the smile comes from? Did Walt find a kindred spirit in this man whose eye I am looking through, a best friend?

Later in life, after the war was a memory the world was trying to forget, when the old men sat in their circle outside drinking warm beer, the kids among them desperate for a seat in the circle, wanting to be men, did they look at Walt and notice something? What only those who know combat know?

After I came home from my very own combat tour, he sat with me in his living room. I sat on a rough and firm couch in their ranch house, stuffed tastefully with antiques on Mission Avenue in Kalispell, Montana looking out over the Lewis range of mountains. I saw those eyes looking east at the great mountains rising north, forming the entrance to Glacier Park past the railroad I knew as a child, the town filled with cowboys and smoke, past the little white house across from the baseball diamond, and saw the same eyes. They were eyes he let me penetrate the history of just once.

Walt assumed the same sideways glance and half-smile, always looking at me, through me to the mountains, to Montana, to a barrier that helped hide the past. We saw beyond the mountains to the Great Plains where someone wishing to be alone always was. We shared stories; at times, his smile darkened and left totally. At others, often when talking about friends, the smile became more than half. The knowing look joined the eyes and they sparked with a life known long before. The close-cropped and now totally white hair showed, slicked back under a tilted cap.

Was this considered an adventure for the young man? Walt, the self-made man. The boy Walt, who was teased as a child. Not knowing how to read, who by sheer will learned his letters. Did he need to leave San Francisco as an adventure? Was it an attempt to prove himself? Was it patriotism?

He found himself the recipient of two purple hearts. I found myself the recipient of a weak form of dysentery, self-loathing, and lost, but otherwise not a scratch. He was himself a survivor of the army's retreat from the Chosin Reservoir. He found cold so complete and intense, his gloved hands and booted feet were frostbitten through. *Ah, is that why his hand was in his pockets.* I guess the tingling was bothering him.

It was an adventure and it wasn't. To this young Walt, the world was something, perhaps an oyster, or the irritant pearl. Perhaps more, a young *Candide* where little was to go well. Stoicism his only true friend. What happened when he came home? He was given a few bucks and a bus ticket and was told to forget it all happened. How could anyone feel at home after leaving their brothers to go to a place where 'it didn't happen'? Similarly, how could I come home? What is home after all? Is it the place we inhabit, or the mindset, the longing, the meditative happiness?

Towards the middle of my last deployment, we were surrounded by so many explosions and gunshots we simply got used to them. We didn't heed the *complacency kills* signs in the base, and in the heat of summer. I wanted to die. It seemed like a good way out of the war. Or, I guess it would be more accurate to say I would be willing to die if it had gotten me out of the hundred and forty-degree madness and purposeless bullshit. I know I was not the only one to have it, because we started to take risks we normally would not have.

I geared up for patrol one afternoon north up MSR Henry toward the main supply route that bisected the city of Fallujah west to east. These two roads were our IED alley, and walking them was rolling the dice. Each time we walked, we winced while passing trash and dead bloated animals. We walked as a squad for a few hundred yards, all spread out so if an explosion hit us, not all of us would be killed. Over the internal squad radio crackled the message:

I stopped. "Uh, Orison, I think I see an IED." I was standing with Orison, my friend and current squad leader, as his RO and the two of us moved up and used our weapon-mounted scopes to figure it out. It was too hot. In the reticle of the scope the waves rose slow and erotic. They waved like dancing transparent women.

"Thoughts?" we knelt, weapon still raised. I was bored. Men and women gave us a large berth but still somehow we could smell them, hear them, see them stare at us with undisguised loathing.

"Damn it, I can't tell." Orison looked at me and smiled. "Wanna go up and see what it is?"

"Sure, why the hell not." I shrugged lazily. The sun sat high and in the heat and blinding light, I didn't really care anymore. We radioed for everyone to stay in place and on security watch while the two of us checked it out. Let me run this past you once more, the squad leader and his radio operator decided to check out a suspected bomb together. This ranked pretty damn high in all the stupid choices I have made in my life. We walked up to it slowly, slightly spread out in some attempt to, I don't know, correct the mistake we made. Traffic avoided us and the road. People looked down at us from balconies, their arms rested lazily on concrete arches, a Gauloises cigarette slowly burning, untouched between two fingers. All eyes on the two idiotic Americans walking up to a bomb. The suspect was a black garbage bag with wires coming out of it extending down an alley. We walked right up to it, and I kicked the bag a little. It was more of a nudge, and I felt something soft. "This was dumb," Orison slowly said, making every word its own sentence. We looked at each other and smiled nervously. Within seconds, our courage melted and together, and without a word we ran back at full tilt giggling like children.

Like we should have done in the first place, while panting for air and wiping sweat from my helmet brow, I called EOD, and we waited in position for several hours until the harried and weary men lumbered up to us in their specially equipped Humvee. I was always jealous of the EOD teams. They had no masters and did what they wanted, jumping from one IED to the next. They wore bits and pieces of uniforms. This team drove down the road at a canter, easy and slow. We provided security as three jumped out, no weapons, no body armor, just filthy t-shirts and three ball caps. The hatchback of the armored Humvee opened to reveal a command center of computers and boxes. Some minutes later, the skeletal robot rolled its way down the same road I ran, and did so without shaking, nervous laughter, or angst. This far more professional robot discovered in an instant that I had run away from trash. EOD blew it up just for fun. The robot arm placed a block of C-4 explosive on the trash and with a remote detonation counted down. "Fire in the hole, fire in the hole, fire in the hole in three, two, one." The wave covered us, and chunks of dirt and road and house and trash rained down on our helmets. I wish I took more pictures on my last deployment. I have a few bomb craters, rifles in them for perspective. I have very few of me in my full panoply. If I'd have taken one that day, I would have resembled shade more than a person. My sun-browned face white with dust and salt sweat lines. My desert utilities white, dust-blown, torn, stained, and soft as silk.

Looking back at pictures it was my eyes that surprise me the most. They were the only thing that contained life. The body moved as if commanded externally, but in pictures my eyes held hope. It is almost opposite to the same eyes I saw in Walt. His eyes in life and in photographs seem lost and without hope. Lost to me are the times Walt would have given up. I will never hear the stories where he accepted death as a natural course of life.

I know in his eyes he accepted it more than I had, but I will never hear how he would have shown it. I wonder if he had stories like mine, unexploded ordinance, standing high and tall in the middle of an attack, defying the enemy hordes. Now, the only stories I have of young Walt are those I imagine from photos. Good thing my imagination is good.

A VISIT TO THE DOCTOR
Al Anbar
March, 2004

One morning, I think it was the third in our journey south from our home base in central Al Anbar, to Fallujah in order to help out in Operation Vigilante Resolve, a FRAG order cracked over the loudspeaker attached to the radio. *Gunfighter Three, this is Gunfighter Six, stand by for FRAGO.*

Roger, standing by, the lieutenant called back while the twenty-some-odd Marines in the AAV craned our necks to hear.

Your platoon is to move to the grid, Papa, November 34564326, break. You will move on foot to a High-Value target's location and attempt to apprehend the target for questioning, break. The target is a doctor suspected of providing care for the enemy fleeing the cordon around Fallujah, break. A possible enemy in the area, how copy? He finished copying down the order and popped his head around the aluminum corner to the vehicle commander and the amphibious vehicle stopped abruptly.

"Punch out security, squad leaders, on me." The lieutenant squatted on the roadway and from a distance, shared five minutes' conversation with the platoon's sergeants and corporals. They nodded and scattered.

Third platoon was ordered to disembark the AAVs and make our way by foot several clicks (a thousand meters per click as the crow flies) to the east to check out some intel we received concerning a doctor treating insurgents at his home who were wounded in the fighting in Fallujah who happened to escape the fighting. We were to find out the validity of these claims, and if they were true, detain the man, and destroy any weapons and medical equipment we found.

We geared up and in double files moved out over a dike and across a multitude of fields green with the spring sprouts. The dust rose as we walked, turning around slowly every dozen steps or so the swiveling back again. The dust billowed up and settled on our clothes and caked them in a brown residue and settled on our skin and became part of us in the early morning. The beauty of the fields on the other side of the dike, with the intense green shoots contrasting the tan and dusty dikes above them and the rows of date palms in the east below which the sun was trying to peek through took my mind off of the weight. And back to another place wholly separated from war and strife. The shadows that were desert and fighting replaced for the briefest break from the real nature of the world. It was a beauty transcending beauty.

Walking through knee-high sprouts brought an almost religious understanding of the world. My right hand came off the rifle and down at my side, swinging to and fro in the grass as we made a shortcut through the field, the stalks rippling in my fingertips. Unfortunately, those times never lasted. Most often, they were but fleeting glimpses into what life would have been like before the fall of man and the beauty of Eden. But this was Eden; it was where civilization began, and we traced our roots thousands of years into the past, their heroes and kings and gods still a part of us, immortal, transcendent through the ages and dogmas. I felt at home because I was home, a long past mitochondrial home that was feeding me, showing me that I didn't have to hate, I didn't have to fight, I didn't need to keep distancing my soul with black veils of pain and suffering.

As my feet stepped one after another, and the morning dew soaked my boots, socks, and lower pants, I smiled as I struggled to keep pace with a fast lightly moving platoon who were unencumbered by either seventy extra pounds of grenades and rockets or mystical theosophical moments of ecstasy that, fully over, weighed extra heavily on my shoulders. We slogged on, and I struggled to keep pace with the others, but I did so. My boots collected muck and we dislodged much of the harvest from the field as the sun rays sat lightly on the heads of wheat, staying with them as the lightest breeze made the wheat dance and sway. I was out of myself and moved on until the field ended and the desert began.

Almost immediately, as religious experiences play out, the feeling left me and I was back in Iraq, on my way to Fallujah about to destroy another's livelihood.

My purpose that day was not to enjoy the sunlight on the wheat. The real reason for my visit came into sight shortly after the field. It lay in a two-story house in a grove of trees, nestled almost perfectly and quietly. I was sure his views in the early morning were spectacular. Beyond the house were outbuildings for animals and equipment. His donkey grazed while tied up to the wall of the first outbuilding, and there was a calf gently munching on hay nearby. They had no idea. Naturally, the doctor was out. We knocked for a few moments, absurdly, like polite guests until possibly around the fifth knock and then kicked the door in. Simultaneously, the other team came in the back entrance and there were other teams surrounding the house to stop any runaways. The assault teams from third platoon's men quickly searched the house and found it empty, but not long abandoned. There were surgical tools in one room and a recovery room in another. It was clear the doctor had been practicing on trauma patients up until recently. We figured he left as soon as he saw the tracks lumbering in columns down the roads. He was one of the smart ones; it was clear he had been treating the injured fighters of Fallujah and Ramadi. The Lieutenant had us pile everything into a large concrete burn pit and set it ablaze. Gurneys, tourniquets, packs of gauze, linen, forceps, all heaped unceremoniously upon the blaze. Nothing escaped our meticulous search.

I still get a sick feeling in my chest when I think of how we tore down this man's life and livelihood.

Our time at the doctor's was short. The fire burned down and we stopped trying to ride the donkey and calf. We left the animals there and formed our two columns, struggling back through the wheat fields to the vehicles. Somehow, I do not remember the fields in the same light as I had before, on the way, and I suppose that is probably a sign of something. It, however, was still different, and there was no going back to the morning light playing across the wheat.

ELECTRICITY
Fallujah, Late March 2004

We saw pictures in the *Stars and Stripes* newspapers that were delivered to us weekly and made their rounds as fast as nudie magazines. Opening the brittle pages that became sun-bleached almost as soon as the desert sun washed over them, I saw a black and white of the Blackwater contractors hung by what I assumed must be legs. At first, I had no idea what was hanging. I had to read the caption. Even on paper, the charred corpses resembled nothing that anyone could recognize as formerly human. I would see the faces of men I knew. The captions never revealed how they met their end, only who they were and where they were from. The rest was left for imagination.

In a small village, we took a few potshots. They were nothing special, in fact, the bullets seemed almost perfunctory rather than lead carrying any hate behind them. But we were hyped on faces and charred bodies and had no time to spare anyone no matter how half-hearted the effort. The drivers edged the tracks off the main road and down into a small valley where a couple dozen houses sat, squat and sad. They looked like the kind that are often forgotten. The Iraqi version of a trailer-park. The vehicles halted in a lurch and the gate dropped fast and hard, burying into the soft dirt of a planted field.

All the Marines ran in teams of three through all the houses. We assaulted house to house, raiding and trashing them all.

I joined in, of course. My team went separate from the rest, wanting our own fun. The three of us started to bust down doors and trash houses. The heel of the boot kicked backward like a horse is the best way to bust down a door if no tools are present. We took turns placing our backs to door frames, winding up, and kicking backward. Often, the doors would not give, and the kicker flailed in quick succession until the bolt broke away. "Back away, my turn," my team leader prodded me with a mocking laugh.

"Fuck you, I have it!" My chicken legs couldn't handle much, but by god I was determined to get this door.

Not wanting to miss any of the action, Sgt. Lynch, one of the track commanders we traveled with, decided to join our team, as he had not fucked shit up yet. We entered a dozen houses one by one, and caused general mayhem, terrifying the populace with gun muzzles in their faces and loud yells for them to keep down or we'd shoot.

Fallujah was evil; we were going to be worse.

I sifted through personal belongings. I threw pillows around rooms to look for hiding spots, pulled open wardrobes and smashed mirrors with my muzzle. I had a good ol' time. Lynch followed me and barked laughter when I shattered the mirror. "Hearts and minds my ass!" I shouted. General Mattis ordered us to "First do no harm," but we were kids and there was a wild streak in us. We knew we would just pick up and leave in at most an hour, so who gave a damn if they hated us when we left. We could justify it by looking for weapons. In the corners of rooms, people cowered and cried. Men looked up at us with well-practiced hatred, the same hatred they showed the Baathists before us, and we looked down at them as conquerors. War had not really changed in the last several thousand years. There will always be the weak and the strong. For the moment, we were the strong and reveled in it.

Our energy waned and we finished our little show of aggression and Lynch left us to man his commander's hatch in his track. Sgt. Lynch commanded the track in front of ours. He was a tall and thin man with legs like a grasshopper's. He was always kind and smiled at everyone, hazed no one, was a leader. In this town, like most we passed through, the electrical wires hung low and usually did not have any protective covering over the copper. The tracks proved to be just high enough that if they were to drive under them, they would catch the wiring, and electrify the crew and all on board. Because of this, the vehicle commanders improvised by finding a forked stick, and using this to heighten the wires, and save all from painful deaths. The yell would be heard as tracks drove down a road, "Mind, wire" echoing down the line.

On this one occasion, however, Sgt. Lynch had the wire slip on him, and slide down the stick, and touched his arm. I didn't see the moment of electrocution. The reaction, the lightning slip through him and out his leg to ground on the track. I heard the helicopter's low whump whump whump as it came flying low and I walked a little faster toward my own track. Rumor spread through the four tracks like a jolt, just like the electricity streaked through Lynch. In a split second the power within his body blew a hole the size of a softball in his lower leg as the electricity escaped towards the ground. He collapsed like wet clay; he lay barely alive. Corpsman ran forward and saved his life. It felt a bit weird that this fun-loving guy was just raiding houses with us. The whump whump whump came closer and I remembered his smiling face laughing, shattering mirrors. Literally moments before, he'd stood behind me and clasped a hand on my shoulder yelling, "Good to go, Marine. Keep it up." Now, he lay on a stretcher hardly alive.

I heard later he recovered in the states. He lived for a while in a veteran's hospital for burn victims in Texas. His wife lived there with him. Because he was not under enemy fire, he would never be awarded the Purple Heart but was nevertheless listed in the *Stars and Stripes* as a casualty. He is a name I recite when I rub the bracelet on my arm. I wish I knew how he is now.

THERAPY
Spokane, 2012

For the second week in a row I forgot to do my homework. I tried to do some in my car when I remembered not doing them. I carried the sheets with me. They stood crinkled and dejected in the book bag I always carried. "Once more unto the breach," I thought walking back down the hallway, scuffing my feet on the worn gray carpet under the off-white walls, devoid of art, just blown up photos of naval vessels and Marines storming beaches. They were cool pictures, but I failed to understand how I was supposed to calm myself while staring at some Marine, weapon low in his hand, clothes tatters, struggling through the sands of Iwo Jima. We sat; I looked sheepish while I filled out the form that just showed me I was depressed and abject. "So, how are your A-B-C worksheets and Challenging Beliefs worksheets coming along?"

"Slowly."

"Paul, I can only help you so much; you need to complete the homework." She turned on her formal mom tone, and her eyebrows dropped. That always got me, and I felt like a child. For a moment, I thought about telling her that I was busy with teaching. I was student-teaching sixth grade English at Moscow Middle School, and as a young teacher, the time needed to plan and grade really was taking up a lot, but that was only half of it. Sure, I was busy, but more than that, I had a revulsion to the sheets that sat on my office desk, pen resting on them in the same position it had days before. I was loathe to work on them, especially the Challenging Beliefs worksheets. These were not simply "Identify problem thoughts" kinds of sheets, but more deep drilling ones that forced me to challenge myself, and really, it was easier to just go with it, and let the emotions pass after my thoughts created the problem.

It was easier to sit in the issues that plagued me. I mean, did I really want to change? It's not like I was some monster.

"Paul, we have had many conversations throughout the weeks since we started CBT. We are now more than halfway through the 12-week program and honestly, I would love to see more progress than I am seeing. I think you are coming along, but are quite resistant to the worksheets and homework. Why?"

I sat a little ashamed, a little deviant. "Honestly, I do think about them. The other day, I was in class. It was a math class. I did poorly on the assignment, I mean poorly for what I usually get. I got up and left in the middle of class. Out of the room, I began to think it all through. My failing in my mind didn't have to be the end of the day. In the past, I left and went home and didn't leave for a few days. I sat and thought through the process. I did the A-B-C in my mind. So, I am doing them, I just am not always *doing* them."

"You must do them more on paper. I need you to do more. I want you to physically work on them because the act of writing is a way to think critically through the event by the physicality of writing. But, enough of that. How are your trauma accounts coming along?"

"I have been writing them. I am working on the day I lost Dobbins and the other four. I am kind of stuck on that part. It's hard for me to remember, let alone get it all down. I am stopping a lot." There was a fear I had, almost like a stuck point. I knew that if I wrote down the stories, that's what they would become. What if I wrote them wrong? Would it change the memory? Would it then be my memory, or a made-up story?

"That is fine. I want you to work through these in your head as well as on paper, but I want you to think about your stuck points while you are at it. Think of your challenging questions. When you hit a potential stuck point, think through these questions, and challenge yourself and your thoughts." She handed me the paper. On it were ten questions to think through. While the format of the A-B-C worksheets was more fill in the blank and less thought-provoking, the questions were more focused forcing me to think. I could do this.

1. What is the evidence for and against this idea?

2. Is your belief a habit or based on fact?

3. Are your interpretations of the situation too far removed from reality to be accurate?

4. Are you thinking in all-or-none terms?

5. Are you using words or phrases that are extreme or exaggerated?

6. Are you taking the situation out of context and only

focusing on one aspect of the event?

7. Is the source of information reliable?

8. Are you confusing a low probability with a high probability?

9. Are your judgments based on feelings rather than facts?

10. Are you focused on irrelevant factors?

Thinking through the list, I had to answer yes to all the above for many of my interactions and thoughts that troubled me. Now, when I do poorly on an assignment or task, what conclusion was I jumping to? Was I thinking in all or none terms? Was this the end of the world for me? More troubling than that, however, begged why I acted in this way to so many situations that were really small issues in the grand scheme? They were peanuts compared to problems the rest of the world dealt with. Why did they hit me so hard, and the larger problems washed off my back like water? I looked back to the pictures of Iwo Jima. I wondered if the veterans of that and other horrific battles struggled back home with feelings of failure of loss anger and a lack of understanding themselves? The answer had to be a resounding yes. I wondered if some of them went through the same trauma therapy I was going through.

A WELCOME HOME MORTAR
2005 Al Amariah,
Zaidon Region South of Fallujah

Early in June 2005, we were ordered to move from downtown Fallujah. We were to leave hard-won relationships, promises and familiar faces for a new area entirely, well, not entirely. So, we packed up our ammo, porn, and portable shitters and lumbered down south thirty kilometers to our new home of Al Amariah. The company was to going be split up into three small platoon-sized bases. Weapons and third platoon were to occupy Amariah while first and second would take over Ferris Town, the same Ferris Town from a year prior. Company operations set up south of Ferris. Our new compound comprised three small buildings surrounded by a tall wall. Recon built three posts, and we immediately enhanced them from something that looked like a blind man drew to a respectable and defensible post. On day one, a team of third platoon's men went out with Recon to try and understand the area. Within an hour of their stepping off, the hidden enemy struck with mortars. The third platoon was now down two men.

I went on post with the old man of our platoon—a veteran of the Somali campaign and former Detroit ironworker who left the foundry to rejoin the Marines and fight with us. We lay in the small circle of sandbags watching the mortars drop to our north and the helicopter come in for a medevac. After an hour chatting about back home and lobbing our half-filled piss bottles at working Marines from the second story, the battalion gunner came and made his rounds. (The gunner is a highly respected warrant officer—a mythical superposition of officer and enlisted—this man is the battalion's tactical and weapons expert. Becoming a gunner was an almost impossible task of memorization and godhood.) He popped his head up to our post and exclaimed, "Holy shit, this is a fucking worthless post. I guess recon does what they want. We're going to have to fix this problem, won't we gents?"

Before we could really even straighten up from slouching and pretend like we cared, I heard something I had never heard except out of Hollywood movies. With a long and high-pitched scream that started from the horizon and rushed into our position, into my soul, artillery rounds, real artillery rounds, screamed and smashed into the town seven hundred yards away. The scream was unmistakable, and I yelled down to the men below us "INCOMING!!" I drew out the last 'I' as if I could not move off the word. Saying it gave me comfort in my panic.

The gunner yelped at the whistling scream and jumped off the ladder, bolting to the command post in another building. The ground around us shuttered from the force of iron and explosive as a jet of earth and crop and house, and hopefully not people but hopefully the enemy, jetted up into the air like a geyser. Three more rounds slapped the ground causing the ground to rocket upward. Below me, I heard a high-pitched voice. "Do they know we are almost danger close? Someone get on the horn and stop that battery!" The ground settled, and the helicopter took back off carrying our wounded and the rest of the recon team humped back to base shaken, but glad to be leaving.

We wasted hours in full gear in front of the base filling sandbags. Thousands of sandbags were brought in and dropped in great pallets. The pallets sank into the soft earth with the weight, and protection became our feasible goal. Where the hell was I, and more importantly, why was it so normal? Sure, the artillery was not an everyday occurrence, but the rest was normal. We went day to day, week to week, and the miles of patrols added to an uncountable morass of moral ambiguity and internal crisis.

Just a few days earlier, we sat in a courtyard in downtown Fallujah along the MSR and nodded thanks muttering *Shukraan, Shukraan* while trying not to look at their wives for fear of offending our hosts. They were all smiles ,and we walked with them through their houses holding their hands and not worrying about what it meant to hold a man's hand. I was happy. We stopped at their copy of the Koran in their prayer room, the room they were letting us stay in when not posted on the roof and a look of love and longing drifted over our host's face. Through the translator he told me that gold clad copy was passed down from father to son for many generations. He was the fifth to have it, I think. We sipped chai and laughed as their children played around us and asked us about our gear, looked at our maps, sat on our laps. They took a risk helping us, taking us in, swallowing what they heard about us in order to show charity and kindness. Would that care have happened in America were we the invaded instead of the invader?

This little town was situated right on the Euphrates and in the midst of beautiful and fertile farming land. We would end up patrolling through grapefruit orchards, date palms, small farms, and other aspects of life we lost centuries ago. We would collect grapefruit, feasting on it until the juice stained the kevlar throat protectors and dripped down the front of our armor. We would take handfuls back home to the Marines on post. We walked the streets downtown, waving at kids who waved back. The local women came to meet us with armfuls of bread still warm from their tandoors. We bought live chickens, wrung their necks and plucked them. We paid in American dollars and the goods began to come more frequently, as did the sickness—that is until we got used to this better way of life. The sickness did not come as often anymore. Once we left Fallujah city, most of it disappeared. The chickens turned gold over the campfire that we made every night. We stared into the flames and listened to the ghostly call to prayer floating like heat waves. We found more IEDs than ever, and our base was attacked several times, leaving us to scramble for weapons and gear as the M-240s barked rhythmically from the posts. But overall, the American dollar bills we flooded the economy with bought us sympathy and, at times, legitimate friendship from the locals. We replayed the scene in time, holding hands with our hosts, walking with them, being served by them, them protecting us from neighbors and other foreigners. How can a person hate those who are generous and kind and loving without any reason to be other than sharing similar DNA?

THERAPY

I am going to do something about this. At this point, we are several weeks to the end of the behavioral change classes and it's time to start thinking about how I have changed thus far. "Paul, what I want you to do is this: take a break from triggers and think about how you can put into words your change. We are almost done, and I think you have made real progress—at least from your homework—I want a final impact statement. I want you to go over the change on paper. Make it real."

Social convention says insanity is trying the same thing time after time expecting differing results. I wander and wander looking for somewhere, some nook where I can hide. Each day I look in vain for somewhere I am comfortable and can study without looking up at every random movement caught in my peripheral vision.

I look for that place, and state of mind where my heart doesn't skip a beat when I hear Arabic in the crowd. I want to smile and enjoy the lilting flow and music of the language. Deep down, I love the poetic movement. Each word flows into the next, a story in and of itself. Each word a burble of a stream flowing against rock and branch forming something beautiful. I want to enjoy it.

Glossary of Stuck Points #8: **Something out of my control is dangerous, so I need to worry about it even though I cannot change it.**

Each day, I try a new spot, only to get up and move on to my perpetual wandering shortly afterward. That's the funny thing about PTSD. In my case, if I am sitting in a crowd, I look, judge, and worry. When I get up to wander, I am fine. When there are movement and control, I am fine; when something happens and I cannot see an endpoint or manipulate the events, I am lost. I am a wreck. The stress associated with no resolution is a silent killer. I guess the smart people at the VA are right. Doing something, anything, does alleviate much of the problem. At least it lets me run away for a while, which they are not happy to hear about, but I am not perfect.

Now, physically back home for good, I feel like I am in more danger than over there. I have long since forgotten which is a dream and which reality. I think this is a reality, but what is reality without people shooting at you, bombs going off, and constant violence? What is reality without my brothers?

When I first came home, I lived in the city and was lost in a whole host of sniper hides, murder holes, bottlenecks, and wandering suspicious vagrants. They shook their tin cans at me, saying they were veterans. Hearing this, I always have to look into their eyes, and if nothing else ask,

"Oh yeah, which unit?" most of them claim to be special forces, or SEALs, or some other unlikely specialty. There are a few who, when I meet their eyes with mine, we both know. I look down and see the black or silver engraved band on their wrist. I know the struggle. I recognize a brother or sister when I see them. And I try to help. We are both homeless.

No matter what, though, the thought is always in my head, swimming nervously in the deep end.

Could they be suicide bombers? I would be without a hiding spot to wait out a counter-attack or a weapon to push through.

At the VA office, they taught me coping techniques, breathing exercises, and stress management theory. They want me to breathe in a circle. They suggest I move beyond challenging my beliefs and confront my problems head-on. They offer to give me sleeping pills to help me cope with nightmares. What they don't understand is my sleeping dreams are that of decision and understanding. I can control them. I dream of war and torture, blood and hatred, but I have a weapon, I move in toward the sound of gunfire and can confront my enemies in my sleep. I cannot do that in reality. Well, I could, but they would put me away and tranquilize me until I am still as a tree. Why would I want to give up my dreams? It is the waking life that is a nightmare. Sometimes I think they want too much. Moving to North Idaho in late 2009 seemed like a big step. Small town life provides a hiding spot where I can slow down and calm down.

Why do I dart my head around in circles with ever-searching eyes? My therapist says it is the anticipation of a battle that remains in our minds. It turns the world into a battleground of nerves and tension. Veterans often search windows, rooftops, trash on the street, dark alleyways, the homeless resting on the building steps and ventilation grates, and the people simply passing by with bread under their arm sticking out of a shopping bag. Somehow a non-hostile baguette becomes a multitude of possible weapons. The brain never really comes out of that hyper-alert stage. I hear it has something to do with a chemical imbalance. At least that's what I took away from my early sessions.

I don't think it is the loud noises that get me; I respond to them, just not appropriately. I don't dive under the tables. I don't freak out and run away. My heart goes off like an Olympic sprinter, my breathing adjusts itself to shorter quicker movements, and all I want to do is fight back. The problem is, there is no one to fight. It would make me feel better to beat up the frat boy who is staring at me, but the feel of handcuffs behind my back isn't my favorite. I am expected to respond normally to the server dropping the tray or the van that backfires. I try to tell my body to respond normally, and it usually listens, but habits take a while.

I've, been home for fifteen years now. Each month that passed in the early days brought me news about my old unit. Who died today in Afghanistan, how many Taliban had they killed? Just how miserable are they? Now, I get news on my Facebook feed about suicides. I see the faces once more, changed over the years, sometimes more scarred and pained than I remember them when they were eighteen and carefree, ready to take on the world. They stood toe to toe with the worst threat the world has at this time and survived. They came home and couldn't take life without brotherhood and stress. We cannot take life without decision and action. They leave wives, girlfriends, mothers and fathers and children. They also leave brothers behind who read about their deaths the day after on their Facebook feeds.

Why was I sitting at home with half a bottle of good scotch—the rest would be gone that night—while they drank warm non-alcoholic O'Doul's? When I talk to the people at the Veterans Hospital, they teach me about my survivor's guilt. They say I've got it bad. But that will never change. They say no matter how much time I spend in-country, and how many battles I fight, I will always have it.

I sit back in the uncomfortable chair and listen while they teach me techniques to bring my anger level down when triggered. I have had hours of instruction, but once I'm triggered, I forget all my techniques and go into my *battle zone*. The next time I see a face I recognize on the news, I feel myself sliding backwards into the zone we talked about. That is a bad place to be.

I'm confronted on the street by a man who wants to thank me for my service. All I can do is drop my eyes and meekly take his hand. How do I answer his thanks? *My pleasure? No Problem?* Hell no, I should say *thank the dead*, or *don't thank me, I gave up the cause after four years. I'm just a pussy*. Once our hands break apart, I look up and his ball cap says in red and gold that he is a Marine who fought in Korea, the Chosin Reservoir. Great, even worse. A man who really should be thanked somehow thinks what I have done is great and important. I wasn't fighting hundreds of thousands of North Koreans and Chinese. I fought ghosts and whispers. I fought myself. I fight myself. As he walks away, I am compelled to run back to him and thank him. I do so with my mouth screwed up into a serious straight line. My eyes are a little watery. He blushes and doesn't know what to say. We part ways in mutual confusion and (I'm sure) mutual internal conflict. For neither of our wars were to "safeguard freedom of Americans." He fought to hold back communism and keep trading partners alive; I, for oil.

I have resolved myself to the fact it is normal to not wake up from nightmares anymore. It's strangely satisfying to mention this to the therapist. When I see new ones, I use that, and my death camp story to test their reactions. Will they be a good match for me? They offer me pills right away. Not a good match. Next please. They want to talk about it, ask questions, satisfy my selfish need for a story? A keeper.

I find it fun to be with my friends in my dreams, some of whom I can never talk to anymore. I just wanted to say goodbye, but I was fifty miles away and now they can't talk back because they have holes in their heads and their femoral spurts blood on the walls of a surgical room. In my dreams, I can say goodbye. Why would I want to give that all up by taking medication?

I'm told dreaming is a way to unravel your problems. When I first went to the VA about my dreams, they didn't want to listen, but I guess the craziness has become a treat to listen to. That was in 2007, and the first doctor I had to look at my head waved my concerns off and told me to "go home and forget about it all." They all want to hear now.

LEAVING HOME FOREVER
Twenty-Nine Palms, California
February 2004

We left late on the night of Valentine's Day in what was probably the cruelest of jokes for the married Marines. Families, their shadows blurred in the dark, were already half gone from our lives. In the dark, tears still shimmered in the lights of the street lamps and the sniffles of children and young wives and seemed magnified and even lonelier to those of us, like me, who had no one to say good-bye to.

I called my family before packing my phone away with all the rest of my stuff and besides the men standing beside me, I had no one, but they went a long way. Slavens and I sat in the dark on packs lined in perfect rows of green and brown and talked softly with the others, mostly young Marines with no family present. It didn't bother me that my parents didn't fly out to maybe see me for the last time; I knew they loved me. Sitting there with others, I felt more of what old Marines describe as the real family of Marines. We shared in the suffering, we would live or die together, the fellowship was growing exponentially as the lazy wisps of cigarette smoke drifted up in lazy circles and the occasional nervous laugh broke from our tight chests in croaks. It was beautiful, and it still lasts with some of them to this day.

Gunny Dobbins sighed, stood with his family and boomed out that weapons platoon's time came to pack up. "Ok, Gents. Weapons platoon, time to go!" in the dark the voice exploded out like a shockwave. He bent over and kissed his wife, who looked calm, practiced, and confident. He smiled at us all as we gathered around the white busses.

It would not be long before meeting him again. After a long absence of a few weeks in Fallujah, he would pick me up in a great big bear hug.

When it was just us, jokingly I called him dad and all the other platoons looked at Weapons Company with very green eyes. He was by far the best platoon sergeant a homesick eighteen-year-old could have had possibly in the whole of the Marine Corps, and thinking back on that day in early February, I hope I was relaxed by his confidence in us.

As I waited my turn to get on the bus, a line of older women who must have been officer's wives came up to us all in turn and hugged us. On the back of their shirts as they walked away I read "designated hugger" the corps may be full of bastards who want to keep each of us pissed off so we fight harder, but troop welfare is never really skimped on where it matters.

We drove the two and a half hours into civilization again into LA, and we shuffled off early in the morning at March Air Force Base, an old and decommissioned airbase where only the national guard still hangs out in ruins dejectedly clinging on to what is left. This was, however, the place where all chartered airlines would fly in and out to take west coast Marines to war. We began what is called in the military as 'hurry up and wait' time. Briefings in small squads took place as we waited hour upon hour in a hangar. Menial tasks laughingly assigned to us new 'boots' in order to keep ourselves busy and not allow us to gather or become bored. We did this for a whole day while waiting. Twenty-four hours wound past not leaving the hangar except for smoke breaks. Gunny Dobbins made his rounds with our lieutenant, a mustang—a former sergeant—and triathlete who looked hard and battered with striking blue eyes and a shaved head. the two of them ambushed us in small groups and tested us in our preparedness and understanding of the commanding general, General Mattis's, ethos, we called the 5-3-5 cards.

Pre/Post Action: 1. Pre-combat checks, pre-combat inspections 2. Rehearsals 3. Confirmation briefs 4. After-action reports 5. Debrief

Habits of Action: 1. Guardian Angel 2. Geometry of Fire 3. Unity of Command

Habits of Thought: 1. Sturdy professionalism 2. Make yourself a hard target 3. No better friend, no worse enemy 4. First, do no harm 5. Look at everyone as if they are trying to kill you, but do not treat them that way.

The habits, these ethos', created are still with me almost twent years later. Do no harm, sturdy professionalism, and treating people with respect may not have embedded themselves deeply into me as an eighteen year old, but now, I look back and see how they formed the bedrock of my look at the world and at others.

Our NCOs grilled us on these ethos for hours, and we committed them to memory as well as all the other general orders and rules of engagement we had to follow. It was all quite confusing, but exciting.

Our flight came in the form of a charter Boing 787, and we lined up in chalks to board. FAA regulations required us to put all of our knives in the gear under the plane, and they were quite strict about it on the surface. All of our sidearms and rifles stayed slung over our shoulders. We stowed them at our feet all the while wondering loudly to the flight attendants *why not knives?* They looked at us with the standard and general *beats me, you weirdo* look that men get so often from people who do not understand the joke. I took Dramamine and conked out in order to try to erase a few hours of knotted nerves.

A hand on my shoulder. Eyes fluttering open once, twice. Desert air blowing in my face. Still on the plane, a new life, a new world. My team leader woke me and a small smile curled on his lips. I knew some shenanigans were afoot. He handed me a book. "Here, you are our new radio operator for the squad." I think I just looked up at him and answered, "Yes, Lance Corporal" betraying my grogginess. Once the goop was rubbed from my eyes, I understood more of what I was asked to do. What I didn't understand was how this change was about to turn me into who I am, how I was to have access to special briefings, special equipment, special rules others didn't. I was a radio operator now, and I was distinct in my platoon.

THERAPY

I am perfectly imperfect.
I am perfectly imperfect.

The sentence has melded in my brain to become a mantra. Surprisingly, it helps. It somehow makes it ok to fail. I have heard all my life that it is ok to fail. Once in the Marines, failing was unacceptable. Failing meant carrying out black bags stuffed with friends. But I am not there anymore. I cannot think about it that way. I must live in the here and now. The change is hard. It is not easy to reverse a very thorough indoctrination. But, slowly, repeating the mantra, the patina is chipped away. Like an archeologist digging away and pot sherds, with each brush and chip, a little more of the authentic me that would have naturally formed showed itself. It only comes out in small bits. There is no large-scale destruction of the mentality overnight, no *aha*! moment. It takes time, patience and understanding.

"Paul, how are you?" Marla said once again. She rarely deviated her greeting. Once again, I passed the running Marine on Iwo Jima and stared at it. The Marine just hung there. Where was he running to? I walked past and into the office. Paper and binders littered the desk. This was actually strange. The desk was usually immaculately clean. I wondered if the binders were for me. "Paul, today we are going to talk about power and control." I settled in and began to listen. "First though, how has the last week been?"

The last week had been shitty. I worked on the worksheets about changing beliefs and really thought through many of the questions. I tried to work through the pages and questions with each interaction that really made me in a down mood. There were many that week. For some reason, I was just down. It was harder to think positively and retain that discipline. I felt a slide backward. I rarely left the house. I saw passersby walk dogs, talk on cell phones and enjoy life, but I could not join them. I couldn't get myself up. I could tell my wife was struggling with it. I tried to put a good face on for her, but she could always tell. My emotions were out of control. Whatever, I could deal with it. After all, isn't it easiest to just hide the emotions and move on with life? After all, there is a lot about life to deal with without all this turmoil. I must keep remembering I am perfectly imperfect.

CHRISTMAS
December 25th, 2005
Al Amariah

The fire crackled and popped sending wooden shrapnel onto my fleece jacket. I didn't care. I had cigar burns and stains of all natures on the jacket. When a large chunk of black wood flew at me suddenly, I jumped and squealed like hawk spotting prey. Most of weapons platoon sat on stumps, homemade chairs, and a homemade couch that was really just two-by-four slats across a frame with a two-by-four backrest, or stood staring into the flames. It was no good. Each of us tried desperately to recapture that feeling our old selves used to feel back home; the feeling was family. We had family in spades. We, closer than brothers, were family. But there was always some little bit of us that tried to recreate the way it used to be. I think it was a last-ditch effort. We knew nothing was the same, but tried, knowing we would fail.

It was Christmas night, the promised chow that was supposed to come in via helicopter was late—several hours late. Actually, it was so late our platoon Sergeant told us to forget it was actually coming. The batteries on our speakers were actively dying, so Andrea Bocelli slipped from his silky tenor into baritone and as the song slowed to a standstill, he reached a deep and hauntingly beautiful bass with a bravado that tended toward the eternal.

"Somebody please change the damn batteries. It's bad enough already."

"Yeah, I got it." Slavens walked in and soon came out with two more double-A's. "My last ones."

"They'll last the night." Slavens came out with something else. It was a bottle. I already heard the story and knew he had it. I also knew he was saving it for a cold night where any chance of combat was ruled out. Somehow, it seemed to be that kind of night. There were no explosions, no gunshots, not even cars lumbering slowly and squeaking that whine when the breaks were far past gone. Somehow it seemed the people of Al Amariah wanted to give us the night off. Perhaps they saw the depression on our faces that morning when we walked a little dejected through the market, not paying attention to anything around us. Usually we said hello, or *A Salamalekum* while we passed looking at the chickens and bread. We knew many families by then, and when women came up to us with flatbread, it was on this day a chore to smile and exchange American dollars for the pieces of simple bread.

A few weeks before, Slavens was summoned to testify to a military court concerning a man his squad detained. He flew to Baghdad and while there met up with some friendly contractors. State department contractors loved hanging out with Marines on principle. Many of them are former Marines and many others assume (rightly so) that we love getting into shenanigans. In the green zone, anyone with few obligations and lots of training and experience is always looking to get into shenanigans. It's practically a law of physics.

Our deployment was wrapping up, and in a few weeks we would fly to Kuwait and home. Patrols were mostly completed, but to maintain our presence, we kept sending them out. It was third platoon's turn, and all of weapons, besides those freezing in thickly sandbagged posts, sat or stood by the fire. The bottle Slavens had with him made his rounds, and was the first booze most of us coated our mouths with in seven months. I held out a blue enameled cup, an artifact of my former life I swiped from my dad's hunting gear before the deployment. It was among my most treasured possessions. My fingers curled around the honeyed liquid, and I lay my head back looking up at the sky.

I knew this sky. Over two deployments, I spent much time inclined toward it. I knew stars, and when alone on post late at night, I often looked up and stared at them. I made them my friends. The twinkled crisp and powerful reminders of a perfect life. There was no ambient light, and they stood out strong, it was easy to imagine one of them pointing the way home. I drank in small sips coating my mouth.

"So, Warmbier, what are you going to do when you get home?" Smithy, a native Oregonian my former team leader, asked quietly still looking into the fire.

"Oh, ya know." This was often the comment these days. We talked so much about what to do when home, it was hard to think about it and stay sane. Toward the end, the days slowed almost to a frozen standstill.

"Ya know what we should do?" a shadow standing in the back asked quietly. Slowly the murmur of side conversations died down. "I bet LT is missing home. He is on watch right now all alone. Let's go sing him a Christmas carol. Or two." We agreed.

"What songs?" *Feliz Navidad* was jingling on the speakers.

"What about that one?"

"Well, I don't know that song; it's in Mexican."

"Christ, Warmbier, you stupid *pendejo*"

"Just sayin', Magallion. I don't *habla*." Maggie smacked me on the back of the head, and laughed while sitting back on the couch next to me. "It's in Spanish, *l Stupido*."

"Ok, it's settled. We sing this song once, and head back. I think the little LT is sitting in there watching *It's a Wonderful Life* or some shit the poor kid." On the best of days our Lieutenant stood five foot two in boots and looked about ten years too young to command a platoon of Marines. But all in all, he was good. He made good judgment calls most of the time, and cared about us even if he did retain that superior officer class mentality.

We all trooped to the command building which stood a bit to the south of ours. We crowded into the command room, and gathered around the large map table we used for mission planning. On the opposite end of the room against the wall sat all the radio equipment, several large military radios, rows of Motorola walkie-talkies, speakers, a dejected-looking little lieutenant and his computer. He was indeed watching *It's a Wonderful Life,* and with his back to us, face in the corner he looked like an orphaned kid. We turned on the speakers, turned them up to full blast, and as he turned around startled began to sing.

Feliz Navidad
Feliz Navidad
Feliz Navidad
Prospero Año y Felicidad.

I wanna wish you a Merry Christmas
(and so on almost to an annoying point)
From the bottom of my heart.

We smiled, wished him a Merry Christmas, and as he sat there looking mildly conflicted, we all trooped out, stoked the fire, and passed the whiskey.

HOME?
Fall 2004

In the fall of 2004, we waddled in full gear onto C-130s with nothing but our body armor and weapons and we headed home. Our eight-month deployment finished, this desert was to be exchanged for a friendly one in California, and so many months of boredom and misery were supposed to be forgotten, placed somewhere in my brain until the workup for the next inevitable deployment began months later. I was crossing a special line. I was to be a veteran. I was heading home, but it really did not feel like I was going home.

I don't mean *veteran* in the way that implies I am a crazy, old beyond my young years, someone to be scared of, *because he could just snap, man, at like, any time! You can't just turn it off!* –thanks for that stereotype, *Rambo*. I use it in the old way. The pure way. I was a veteran Marine. I was someone who had been to war and came home to lead the next group of young kids, the kind that I was up until months before. Most of my seniors, like Armas, loaded into the plane feeling like a free man whose time in prison was just about over, and it was just sinking

244

in that in a little while, my group, the ones who had been in the corps a little over a year were taking over the training of new men.

Leave came and went. I went home for a month, slept in late, a few times wandered around the perpetually wet concrete making up Portland, OR. I was without a weapon, without armor, without buddies. If I were still in Iraq, the solitude of it all would have kept me up at night. A few times it did. I waited to hear the soft breathing of others next to me, and feel the vibrations of boots walking close every hour, a shadowy figure stooping to wake up the next watch. It was like the dreams where I was naked and did not look at it. I mostly stayed at home, put on a few extra pounds, which my emaciated frame needed.

When my leave expired, I loaded my old Ford Ranger up with everything I needed for a normal life in California, and started the thirteen-hundred-mile drive. By the end of the drive, my back ached, the result of two nights sleeping on the short bench of a truck cab, my eyes hurt, my spirit was depressed and my intestines needed a detox—as evidenced by the myriad fast food boxes on my passenger seat.

Over the years, the workup for a Marine deployment has changed considerably. It all depends on where your unit is going. Iraq was great and all, but I listened to my recruiters who said Marines travel the world. I wanted 2/7 to head to the mountains of Afghanistan instead of one more in the desert wastes. Intel concerning the next deployment spread through the companies like an STD. First, the plan was Northern Iraq, then Afghanistan, then Fallujah again. It really seemed each day some juicy morsel tempted us. I was part of the senior group, and my mind quickly turned from leave to training for the next deployment as well as obtaining the correct gear.

Gear is a very important issue to the Marines, well, to all deployable forces. There is a fine line to walk when it comes to how much to get, and what brands. No one wants to look like some sixteen-year-old who plays too much *Call of Duty* and then begs their parents to give them the credit card so they can play air-soft. When choosing gear, a surprising amount of thought goes into it. What kind of weapon system? Will we have machineguns, or mortars, or rockets? (Surprising fun fact: not everyone had a fully automatic weapon. The so-called *spray and pray* method so popular in under-trained troops is highly discouraged. To keep that down, semi-automatic weapons—one trigger squeeze, one bullet—was the mainstay of the Marine infantryman.) Whoever was unlucky enough to carry one of the Squad Automatic weapons, or SAWs, carried upwards of three to four drums of belted ammo. That is a lot of weight. Perhaps a harness system with a belt would be the best. As a radio operator, I used a harness for some time, and thought it did a great job of shifting the weight of all the gear around.

If you were in an assault team and had an M-16, chances are you would want a simple system that kept magazines, grenades, and an MRE spoon in an easy to reach place. You wanted a chest harness, or to place all your gear on the gear straps of your flak vest. This would keep everything close and allow for quick reloads if action got too hot. You would sacrifice a low profile while lying prone, but goddamn if it doesn't look super cool. At the end of the day, a large degree of what gear you chose was about looking cool. No one wants to operate while looking like a bag of smashed assholes; of course you want to patrol and intimidate the locals by looking like a machine of murder.

Those of us who had deployed before knew that purchasing gear quickly was a high priority. It was really not an option to find something wrong and have to order anything online while deployed to a forward operating base that received mail once a month. On the firing line, there would be (and I assume still is) about two hundred different setups of varying gear.

Depending on where the deployment planned to send men, training doctrine dictated a different workup. If the unit were going to Afghanistan, the men would spend a month in Bridgeport, California attending the Marine cold weather school. If the unit was going to Iraq, there was a conveniently placed mock Iraqi town few miles from my backyard. The unit would build up for four to six months training new Marines, and retraining old, and culminate with a CAX and time at Mojave Viper training center just north of the main base area.

When I went through my first workup in 2004, there was no Mojave Viper. We 'deployed' for two weeks to March Air Force Base in San Bernardino County squatting in rundown base housing. We learned advanced patrolling and how to work with tanks and AAV troop transport. It was staffed by role players who really were Marines waiting to be discharged, and who were looking for a cushy job for the remaining months of enlistment. It rained on us a lot, and did not do much to train me for Iraq. Working up for the second deployment was much different. Mojave Viper just opened for business, and I found myself talking to Iraqi nationals who spoke Arabic and responded to the Mosque's call to prayer.

I don't remember who, but someone offered me the post of assault section leader, which is essentially a squad leader with a better name. I got the post not because I showed real promise, but because no one else wanted it. Never really one for volunteering myself, when all else failed, I thought I would try my hand at it, and see if I could be promoted to corporal. In the end it didn't work. What was interesting was as teachers with a large new group of *boots,* we were supposed to be role models. Looking around at many of my fellow seniors, I saw drug use, alcoholism, domestic abuse, and PTSD. They were calls for help, and there were very few trained to deal with this injury in a manner that made any kind of difference.

The new Marines came to us and inevitably saw what was going on. They dogged our every step, and were quite observant, not failing to see every morning at least a third of the company either still drunk or hungover. One of my good friends even came up to me after one formation where he was late, and said, "Dude, I am so still trippin' balls. The trees were talking to me on the way to base this morning."

"Excellent." What else could I say that would make any difference? "Glad to hear it. You go straight up to your room and hide out till you are ok." I couldn't blame the guy. After coming home and having no purpose, how could some not go to drugs?

In a way, alcohol is a necessary distraction from the boredom of barracks life. More than that, it was our medicine for suffering. Taken in moderation, and with a group, alcohol was the best therapist I ever had. I was still too young to buy booze. Like anything illicit however, it was not too hard to get a hold of, and the MPs who responded to the calls of drunken 2/7 Marines lobbing beer bottles in perfect arc-like glass mortars at the admin Marines just trying to get to their rooms at night. They generally tried to ignore us. Instead of dragging us off to the drunk tank, they stuffed us in our rooms and instructed any corporal or sergeant who was not drunk to keep a lid on us. Many of the MPs just got back from their own deployments, and were just jealous.

The problem still confronted us daily. The new guys, very few of them over twenty-one were watching us and getting drunk on their own. Soon, they would have problems enough to solve with booze. Our platoon sergeant, Gunnery Sergeant Dobbins often went out of his way to hang out with us, sacrificing his Friday evening time with his wife and daughters. He acted friendly, and used the time to become acquainted with the new boots, but I think we all knew why he was taking the time.

He sat with us occasionally, his arms on his knees and listened. That is all he did, and that's what we wanted. Back home, I wasn't about to tell my parents what it was like to hear the mortars inbound, and wonder when they would be plowing into, or near our positions. Mortars move slower than artillery rounds, and do not whine or scream overhead. They simply plummet to earth without any more warning than the thump of leaving the barrel. Similarly, they would never know what it meant to stumble upon a mysterious building that looks like a gas chamber, or a torture house, or to crouch under a rock as rounds erode the sandstone. The only ones who knew were those who sat and met my terrified eyes with knowing ones.

He was one of the only platoon sergeants who came around, and weapons platoon was stronger for it. He discouraged cliques, abhorred hazing, and valued our mental states more than we would.

Michael Tobin sat leaning back in apparent ease. He wore his green PT shirt and blue and yellow Simpson's pajama pants, the same pants every night. In his hand was an oversized plastic cup with frosted sides so only the shadow of contents was visible. He filled it always with the same drink, orange juice and vodka from a plastic gallon jug. Tobin was most likely the world's largest single buyer of orange juice. His eyes were a bit hazy, but rarely ever *seemed* drunk. "Well, I think we are heading to somewhere totally different this time. At least I hope so; Al Asad was damn stupid, except for the CONEX box homes. Those were sweet."

"I'm not so sure, Mike. I think we're going back to Anbar. You've been watching the news, right?" Came a deep voice from the shadows. There were about a dozen around Mike and Dobbins. A few of us muttered our own thoughts at this. Everyone seemed to know we *were* going somewhere different, and had it from some credible source. Most often, it was some company clerk who overheard some Lieutenants talk about it, most often in order to screw with the clerk.

"Does it really matter where we go? Gents, wherever we go, we will look after each other, and do the damn job together." Dobbin's voice was deep and final. His six-foot six frame and loving presence silenced dissent.

"Yes, Gunny," muttered a dozen voices in unison. He pressed this each time we gathered, whether before or after formation. Every day it was about rolling with the punches and doing what it took to get us all home together.

"Let's just hope it is more of a cakewalk than last time." Another bodiless voice sounded off. "I've had my share of fighting I just wanna go over, and have an easy time of it."

"Pussy," called out another in a sing-song mock. Everyone laughed nervously. "You just don't want anything to happen 'cause you are a walking soup sandwich and you're afraid of fuckin' it all up."

Death is not an adventure, at least for those who stand face to face with it. While I came into the corps with a desire to seek adventure. I wanted to grow up, be powerful, and gain strength externally and internally. That all changed. In 2004 and 2005 all I really wanted to do was survive another deployment or two. I wanted to finish up my required time and get out to enjoy life what was left of my life. Existence is fleeting for all of us. Death could come at a moment. Rarely does it come in the shape of a bullet. It is certain, always there, and inescapable. I wanted to come home and extend that life. The only way I could really do that was to make sure all of us watched after each other, and were more than proficient in killing those who intended to kill us. I once had a tough time with the prospect of killing, and how it conflicted with my belief. How does someone do this, and still consider themselves moral? How could I? I am still not convinced it's possible in any case out of self-defense, but what we were engaging in was not that. We were the aggressors to the nation of Iraq. When they shot at us, I shot back without thinking, but what would I do if my home was taken over by a foreign power? I would like to think I would try to repel the enemy.

We trained our men the best we could. We went to division schools—a reapplication of what we learned back in infantry school—we completed our workup for deployment, and we participated in a CAX to retrain ourselves, and set up the structure we would have in Iraq, as well as reinforce our SOPs for contact, ambushes, HVT actions, patrolling, and all other aspects of warfare. This was all good and fair, but also clear that some of our guys were starting to show anxiety for the next deployment. We drank more. We drank insane amounts, actually. We drank almost every night. We drank like we were vacuums. It was a way to decompress and think about what happened as well as what was going to happen as a group. It was a way to ignore the reality of the future and to forget that there could be a future. I sank into times of deep depression. I spent days rarely leaving my room, not talking to anyone but my roommate, and generally being unpleasant.

I did not understand what I was feeling and I didn't know how to ask about it. No one did. We all exhibited anti-social and depressed moments that manifested themselves differently in all of us. Therapy was still a taboo. On top of this, I was nineteen, and not very adept at introspection. I just thought this was normal, and talking to someone about my fears or hatred of life just did not really hit me. I internalized it, and let it out only when I was with others and had been drinking.

Not all was bad, however. I really enjoyed being a section leader. I loved taking care of the issues of my peers and subordinates, and thinking about this later, I think this would contribute to my future desire to teach as a profession. I was never one that put much stock in promotion in rank. I was a lance corporal. Corporal rank was difficult to obtain in the infantry, and with the war, meritorious promotion happened regularly in other units making the quotas fill quite fast. Section leader as an assault man was a billet usually held by a sergeant and when one of my men (a guy senior to by about a year) was about to be promoted to Corporal, I tried to work it out with my platoon leadership that his promotion would not bump me out of the section leader spot. With a promise of this, I gave my signature to his promotion the same day we got a new Lieutenant straight out of the academy. He immediately ousted me and installed the new corporal. I became a team leader, in charge of four men. I could live with this. I handpicked my team, and grabbed men I knew would work well with me.

The time came once again, and, feeling like an old hat at this sort of thing, I boxed up all my belongings, again, and waited for the last remnants of America to fade away in the slipstream of the jet.

We shuffled through customs check-in Kuwait, and nervous hands moved towards smokes, seeds, dip, whatever, and flew to Camp Fallujah. I was actually excited to be here again. I was older, smarter, and understood more of why I was here. I had a smattering of new guys with me, and old brothers that clung to each other. Loyalty was to your squad and platoon. After that in the sphere were the company and Battalion. Finally, the Marines and America took the outer ring of loyalty. The mission, for me, and for us all took the form of bringing everyone home.

I was always taught as a kid, whether by society or family, that service is all about God and country. Growing up in Northern Montana, and then in central Idaho, I was reared in a country that valued its America First ethos almost above anything else. It was all for God and country, and damn it, you better be doing it for the *right* god. *You know the one I mean.* My family never really put pressure on me; maybe they knew where I was going before I did. I did not really believe in the mission America had in the Middle East. I did not, and still do not think we need to be bringing democracy, KFC, southern accents, or Barbie into a tough land with no need for such crutches.

I remembered my interpreter, Mahmud, a former professor at Baghdad University. He lost his entire family to Saddam and was tortured (perhaps in one of Fallujah's torture houses) until he lost most movement in his left hand and the last remnant of hope in his grey eyes. This was about survival and protection. He talked to me in the planning room. "Why are you helping us?" I was genuinely puzzled. Most Iraqis waved, or stood stoic as their feet crumbled under the weight of our vehicles.

"It may not look like it, but I have hope." He smiled and turned to the vehicle, raising one hand for help. He sat and stared unblinkingly at his home, the only one he knew. Even in the depths of misery and uncertainty, he retained some measure of hope. In Fallujah, I never saw any of that.

Golf Company gained the use of a series of three

houses walled off from the city, a place all our own. Marines in the unit that came before us built posts on the walls, and sandbagged windows and walls until it was hardly believable that the structure would not collapse. We set up shop and made this place our own. Pictures out of Penthouse and Hustler went up on walls and in conveniently placed stashes—the kind that arctic foxes make in order to preserve food for harder time. Almost immediately, patrols began.

We flew directly into Camp Fallujah from Kuwait. I and other team-leaders formed the advance party that would slowly take over during the week where both units were in country. The drive from Camp Fallujah was a familiar one. I remembered lumbering in over a year prior to the push through Fallujah. The few of us on the convoy were all there before and knowing eyes smiled back at remembered and rusting hulks of Iraqi tanks, destroyed during the invasion, landforms, that watched the rise of human civilization, and passing a people still suffering under the memory of a man long ago hung by a think rope. There were more moments of uttered, *do you remember...* always followed by silence and knowing nods. We all remembered this push, and at least for me, it terrified me. The prospect of going through it again made me hide my shivers. We drove to a base in the southern half of the city, weapons pointed outward from armored Humvees and waited for the black smoke and bone-jarring tremor of an IED underfoot.

I sat in the back, looking across, toward the side of the road behind Tobin directly in front of me, and he watched my back. We pointed out several areas, which we remembered, and kept our eyes peeled. The last time I saw the city was from the outside. We cordoned the city off in 2004 and watched a forty-hour firefight rage itself unchecked through the city. Smoke billowed up and the chatter of talking machineguns incessant. Now, in the back of the Humvee little kids waved, and old men stood on the side of the highway watching yet another group of Marines march into their city.

On the first deployment, we mostly conducted patrols mounted, which made things much easier. The gear we humped was not as heavy, the ground not as hot, and the people viewed through the bulletproof window of a Humvee, not as hostile. In Fallujah this time, patrols were almost all on foot. We walked on boiling asphalt until our feet turned spongy in wet socks. We shuffled on, ignoring the pain in our bodies, focusing our minds only on the mission at hand, and searching for some enemy. They were out there. Snipers drilled holes into Marines and civilians indiscriminately. "You have to ignore the pain." I kept hearing, "Just keep your head on a swivel."

The patrol leader mapped out a route around a central mission (this could be anything from running an ambush, canvassing local business leaders, paying local leaders and sheiks for the use of their information, or buildings as listening and observation posts, raiding a High-Value Target's (HVT) house, or simply walking around in concentric circles 'observing local feeling toward us' that usually meant finding a shaded spot and laying down in a security circle for hours). Patrols became an opportunity to understand these people as ill-treated, pained, and misunderstood as well as murderous, cruel, and opportunistic. There were many who welcomed us in with traditional Arab charm and hospitality. There were many who defied the fliers and warnings from insurgent cells to offer no aid.

TRUST
August 2005

Glossary of Triggers #9: When I think about what we did to people, I know I cannot trust myself to be a good person.

Late in the summer halfway up the dusty road which separated East Fallujah from West Fallujah, a man stood in the middle of the road with a smile on his face and dust settling on his outstretched arms. "Marines, Marines, come in. Please it's too hot," he filtered the words through his teeth and heavy mustache like baleen in a whale. He was tall and built with that typical male belly pooch so typical of middle-aged men. We often walked past this house on patrol, and on hotter days staggered by without a welcome. I looked at Orison, a Marine I had been with since boot camp, without knowing what to do. In my mind, I ran all the possible scenarios. Ambush chief among them. I looked around at other buildings, looking for a possible sniper hide.

"What do you think, man? Do we trust him?" I stood next to Orison as his RO and quietly we sized the man up.

258

"I don't really give a shit. It's way too hot out here. He is probably fine." He looked into the cloudless sky and then at his watch as if looking for an excuse. It was midsummer and the daytime temperatures routinely soared near one-hundred and forty degrees. At that temperature, trapped in the sixty to eighty pounds of gear we wore, there really was no way to keep hydrated. "We're supposed to talk to community leaders here, and he is a local leader. Let's see what he has for us." Over the internal squad radio, Orison radioed back to the team leaders spread out in the open along the main thoroughfare. "Ok, Gents, let's get out of the sun and talk to this man. We may kill a few minutes."

"Roger."

"Lima Charlie." (Marine for Loud and Clear)

"You got me, Warmbier?" Orison asked without looking. I followed not needing to answer. We both smiled and placed our right hands over our hearts in a sign of peace. "Au-salam Alaykum." I started to enjoy saying it to people on this tour. I felt less like an infidel invader and more like a helper. To me it really meant *I'm here to help you, what can I do?* It also meant, *I come in peace. If you don't, I won't lose any sleep after I put three bullets in you.*

He replied, "Alaykum Salam" in slow and dulcet tones that sent the gravity of the expression home. His voice was deep and husky rolling the short phrase out under his mustache slow and thoughtful. We all crowded at the door and followed this man into a large courtyard bricked off on three sides with a shade covering. The air hung thick with hot flowers and the exotic scent surprised me. We all sat on white plastic chairs, the kind that broke immediately after bringing them home from the store. His wife, wearing the traditional Hajib or upper body and face-covering smiled and brought us all tall cool glasses of Tang. Water beaded down the glass and over my fingers sending prickly stabs of pained confusion through my skin. We all looked at each other. Poisoned? Euphrates water? Who cared anymore, and with the others, raised my glass to our host. Not even back home would I be greeted with such neighborly care.

I knew there were very few places in America where strangers still invited others in on hot days with lemonade and a smile. Back home, people locked their doors when someone new came, scared for some religious solicitation. Back home, we have it all wrong.

On that dusty street, one man and his family risked their lives for a haggard group of men noticeably slouching as the sun pressed down.

The man raised his glass to all of us, and only after we gulped the cold liquid did he smile at his wife and take a drink.

Fallujah is easy to find on Google Earth. Obviously they do not feature a street view but from an aerial one, I can pick out intersections that I still recognize. That is probably due mostly to having a map in my hand most patrols. I know the aerial view of most buildings in southern Fallujah. Sometimes late at night, several fingers of whiskey in my glass and all the lights off, I hunch over my computer screen and stare at intersections and houses. I found our old base recently. I stared at its palatial expanse of rooftop broken in the exact center for an open-air courtyard.

I sometimes like to think I could zoom in close enough to see this man looking up at the drone. In his hand is a glass of cool tang. If I could zoom closer, I would see the condensation bead up on the outside of the glass and slowly drip onto the concrete of his courtyard and he would be content, a smile branding out of his moustache. His wife would be sitting next to him and all around him are ghosts people who left a part of themselves in that house and in that country. I am there. I smile and enjoy the cheap plastic chair and the moment of rest. The part of me that will always be in Fallujah hangs out there often. He always has a glass waiting for me and a soft loving look at his wife who dutifully brings us rest.

That evening we rested, he mentioned in passing that we could use his roof for observation posts. He liked us, and was not afraid of the repercussions he told us. I would be terrified of helping us, for the penalty was usually death. We used his roof not a week later. Two men lay on their bellies looking over the roof palisade while the rest slept. I didn't. I stared at the night sky. The stars in Iraq are like nothing I have seen since. The population of pinpricks is infinite. I loved to stare at the sky. I still do, but have yet to capture the same awe. In the morning, his wife brought us a metal plate the size of a table. The Tang was there, warmer than the chill blanketing us in the early morning light. Next to the pitcher of Tang sat a teapot of steaming chai, and a dozen fried eggs. I could have cried.

I used to look at Iraqis like many eighteen-year-old conservative men did at the time. I didn't look at them as anything. In reality, they were gods and goddesses of hospitality. The men hid their smiles behind bushy mustaches and the women behind veils but occasionally the smiles stood out stark. I wanted to protect these people and this family.

We left them and paid American dollars for the use of

their roof and the food. I wanted to give them more, but we had only a little. To them though, the few dollars we left were a small fortune. We thanked them and swore to protect them if we could. I said I would never forget their kindness. I haven't.

LIVES RIPPED AWAY
Fallujah, Soda Factory
December 1st 2005

Shrapnel ripped through bodies in the winter morning. Toward the end of the eight-month deployment, while America was worried about domestic spying and folks were worried about having their emails read, though I am sure they should be much more worried about it now, a bomb went off under the feet of a whole platoon of Marines. In an instant of nothingness and dust, several expertly placed IEDs flashed upward as the electrical signal from a trigger device surged forward sending an explosion through sand and rock and out at over five thousand feet per second. Many of them felt nothing as they became memory. The metal shards burst from the ground before the explosion eviscerating everyone nearby, before the blast was even registered by the surrounding Marines. They were in formation and could not have known what was happening. The flash went by, up and over the men so fast the fireball and shrapnel came, singed hair and burnt sweat and dust-covered but now blackened and crisp skin. The shrapnel tore bone and limb, severing flesh from already lifeless and stunned bodies. The men posted away from the platoon, on security flattened their bodies instinctively when the airwave sucked air from their chests and the sound wave passed over them, deafening the unsuspecting.

They were all unsuspecting.

In the minutes that passed, some, disbelieving, sat there and squinted through the dust for the lifeless forms. I imagine the screams came through the buzzing in their heads in time. Some men stood in the dust, some knelt crying, panicking trying to find someone to provide aid. Echoes of "Corpsman Up!" would have rung in the courtyard over and over. In time they died out and the men became hoarse and slumped over, too exhausted and in disbelieving shock.

Ten men died including the man for whom the formation was called. Ten young men died and ten families spent Christmas and the New Year receiving folded flags and weeping into the shoulder of anyone who had a vacancy. Blue stars in windows became gold and the oldest tradition of mankind carried on without a hitch. One whole company was deemed unfit for duty as there were many wounded who needed caring for physically as well as the men who were simply pulling security. I was busy throwing rocks at Slavens instead of watching a city that would rather pretend the Americans in tan were nonexistent or dead.

I was a dozen miles away on my own base and heard the blast. I heard the blast and thought nothing of it. Blasts were more than common in and around Fallujah back in 2005. Fallujah was doing well under Saddam, or at least the Baath supporters were doing well, and there were many of them in Fallujah. Saddam considered this his comfort zone. So, when I heard the blast that destroyed so many men in a measure of time so minute that conceiving of it is difficult—I mean, we measure in speeds so great most high-speed cameras cant capture the moment of detonation—I thought nothing of it and continued doing whatever I was doing. We heard the names of the dead shortly after the incident, and remembered many friends, or acquaintances, or just people we once shared a beer and stories with. The Marine Corps is, after all, a fairly small place. It is not small enough, however, that I may know your friend's brother's cousin who was once a Marine, so don't ask. When this happens all communication with the outside world is shut off. We may know the names of the dead, but the public, not even their families would know for a while. Satellite phones were confiscated, mail outbound was halted on the specific unit, and the internet was turned off for all but the most important communications. I will say that the military is determined to be the first to offer condolences and make sure it is done in the right manner.

Lance Corporals Adam Kaiser, Andrew Patten, John Holmason, Robert Martinez, Craig Watson, David Huhn, Scott Modeen, Corporal Anthony McElveen, Sergeant Andy Stevens, Staff Sergeant Daniel Clay were all killed in that one blast. There were many others wounded that day both physically and emotionally. It is fairly rare anymore that in one day, and in one attack the Marines suffer such casualties. This was, needless to say, truly catastrophic, I remember hearing it was all over national news and I can only imagine what my parents thought when they saw on

CNN. In fact, it was for quite a while the single bloodiest day in Iraq since the last major offensive against a fortified city. Not something really worth being known for. When I heard it, my ears pricked up, and then dropped, my hands trembled, faces flashed before me, and I zoned out, listening to life continuing all around me as if almost a dozen men had not lost everything.

TO KILL
2007-2009

I have never killed anyone; at least, I think I have never done so.

Several times, I shot at a locality where people were shooting back. Several times, I listened to other people as they wept into their hands about watching blood drip from the opening they caused, the blood seeping into the sand. The sand, soaking the viscous fluid hungrily, somehow the desert sand was never satiated.

I dream about it regularly.

<u>**Glossary of Stuck Points #10 and 11:**</u> **I failed to kill any insurgents or foreign fighters and by doing so, I have let my men down, there was no vengeance. Marines are Marines when they have killed. I am no Marine, no warrior, no soldier.**

Most nights, I watch blood slip casually out of bodies to be swallowed up by the sand. I see faces of those who are no longer tangible, simply memory in none but a few minds. I say their names aloud, wondering if I and my brothers are the only ones who remember they existed.

When talking to someone who is not a veteran, it is the second question I am always asked, immediately following the standard 'so...have you killed anyone?' which is followed always before one can speak with 'what does it feel like?' At this point in the fledgling conversation all I want to say is something like, 'look motherfucker, I may not have killed anyone yet, but am about to!' but which is in reality answered with 'c'mon man, I don't really want to talk about that, please.' Or if it is mentioned by one of my students is more usually answered by 'ok class, there is such a thing as a stupid question. *That* was a stupid question.' These days I make sure the topic never comes up, and if it does organically, I usually make no mention of the Marines. I am sick of the questions.

I am sitting in a bar right now writing. Really, I am sitting in a corner with my head down over a standard pad of paper trying to write. I usually try to avoid this, but am sitting within hearing distance of a new, young, and apparently impervious and infallible army officer who is chatting up a friend. The friend asked all three at a cyclic rate, pounding them out quick and fast with wonder and excitement gleaming in his wide-open eyes. This officer didn't quite know what to say. He looked around trying to hide embarrassment then went a bit red. I waited for his response. I waited for him to start telling stories of war right after stories of officer candidate school. Mercifully, he decided on silence, the haven of modest folk and people who still have some integrity. Had he, I would have had a hard time containing myself. Not sure if I could have.

After 2/7's deployment to Hit and Al Asad in February 2004, we had a rash of alcohol and drug-related problems.

People were getting into domestic disputes, fights out in the town, alcoholic hazes and highs that sent them across state lines on chases with ghosts and random imaginary enemies. One in particular now strikes me as very sad, and at the time made me point and laugh and wonder what drove this man to such lengths of insanity.

We had one guy who seemed normal in formation and when the platoon had training exercises and meets-up outside the barracks rooms. When on leave, however, he would go into town and procure some heavy drugs, I'm talking the worst kind of escape.

One time, in particular, he drove down interstate ten at a blistering hundred miles an hour pursued by the police. There seemed like there was no stopping him until he pulled into a California State Patrol station (I assume to the pursuing officers' collective sighs and astonishment) to run out of the vehicle screaming to the officers that he was being chased by a Mexican gang. There was no gang in reality, but he was so addled by undiagnosed PTSD, TBI, and what was probably an insanely bad trip that he was utterly convinced his life was on the line. Thank god he wasn't carrying a pistol. He was released into the custody of the Marine Corps and came back to the barracks room after some time. His poor roommate had the pleasure of watching him sit by the window with a flashlight cursing and swearing under his breath at the gnomes hiding in the bushes past the window. A few Marines thought it would be hilarious to hide in the bushes and come after him, but didn't really want to be the cause of a double or triple murder, regardless of the hilarity that would have taken place. In 2004 on his first deployment to Iraq he had a few of his best friends blown up in front of him. That might make anyone go batty.

This story, however, I think speaks to the way things were before the modern and very novel approach in mental health that dictates that Marines and soldiers must receive care after and during deployments to avoid such break-downs. So why were Iraq Marines treated so poorly? Commands denied the existence of PTSD, doctors at VA hospitals would turn down clearly traumatized veterans, many close to suicide, because they personally thought that PTSD was either not a real thing, or just a cop-out.

I was lying in bed one night, listening to my wife breathe slowly and deeply. I was awoken by a dream. I was back in Fallujah, I was changed, different, the same, unable to be comfortable back home, unable to find common ground, unable to find purpose. All I could think about is how easy it would be. I added it up the other day, and there have been over thirty suicides from my unit alone in the past twenty years.

That's how it starts, how easy it would and could be. My pistol by my bed and the general warm feeling of safety the cold steel provides. I don't know a single one of us that has given up guns altogether. Holding the steel makes me feel better. It calms the nerves and can make one feel like they are back in. Overall, it is a good thing. I don't think how I would do it, I think about simply how easy it could be. It is just a single movement and a flick of the trigger.

That is all it is.

But hope is also the press of a button. It is calling a friend, admitting to fear, anger, worry, or depression. Late in 2018, I went through another period of time where I fantasized about how better the world would be were I just gone from it. The change it necessitated was stark and drastic. Marriage counseling, personal counseling, daily meditation, exercise, more time with the family and less time agonizing of the dumpster fire that was my job. All these drastic actions led to a change which helped me do one thing: I sold or gave to my dad most of my guns, keeping only the favorites, those that do not tempt me, the fine Spanish 20 gauge side-by-side and the deer rifle I got on my confirmation day. Those are tools, not toys. They do not comfort me, or call to me to press them against my skin.

THERAPY

I sat on the same chair as before and was happy to leave the waiting room. She sat across from me, like always, and smiled. "Paul," Marla sighed the type of sigh that is not supposed to be sad. She smiled as she did so, and I somehow felt that she was helping carry my weight. She knew it too. Her sigh told me she was happy to carry a small portion of my burden, and it was this understanding that kept me coming back. More than anyone else, she did more than instruct and reshape thought, she listened without connection or judgment, and let me spill all the brutality, despair, fun, and downright insanity of war. I didn't tell my wife these things because I was afraid of what she would do or say. Marla was safe. "Paul, today is the day. We have completed all the weeks of behavioral modification training and I want to hear what you wrote this week." I wrote down a statement the day before. It was a moment of clarity and honesty I was still uneasy with. I was not sure I believed what I wrote, but it was a start. It was a form of Dr. Jekyll in me desperately trying to talk Hyde off the ledge.

I sighed myself, long and deep and took the breath as

if it were my last. I could feel the air moving through my lungs And I focused on it, hoping I could remain in that second forever and not speak the words I wrote. While writing them I recognized I would be giving up a portion of who I was by airing them. Speaking something aloud is a form of acknowledgment. It is a recognition and it gives the words life. Speaking them allows them to be more than thought, and even though I feared who I had been, there was still a little part of me that didn't want to fully let that go. I opened the red notebook and slowly flipped through the pages. She did not speak. She let me go as slowly as needed because perhaps she knew I would have to read.

The words came out slowly, quietly, almost a whisper. As they came, they became louder until I was speaking in a full voice, not confident or secure, but moving.

I believe now that though these incidents were traumatic for me, and shook many of my beliefs, they no longer have to be debilitating. There are many aspects of my life which I believe the events influenced, such as my self-image and how I view the world. Additionally, my views of control and power, facet and trust were impacted, molded, and contorted out of context and out of recognition.

Concerning self-image, that skewed perceptions after the fact have been downplaying the importance of the Job that I played in the events and turning my success into abject failure. Concerning any king of failure at all I equate any failure or set back to the utter failure in myself. I understand now that in reality, how I responded after several of the major events in my story in no way should reflect negatively on myself to myself. I have no need to punish myself for anything beyond my control and at the deepest level, this was beyond my control, ultimately I have had to rewrite my understanding of failure and what constitutes that as well as how I should react respecting how I feel about myself have come up.

Concerning control, I believe issues relating to needing to be in control of myself, others, and my surroundings are the heart of my pain. I believe that the incident helped to encourage the belief that I need to control others and myself which is unrealistically a matter of life or death in this new world I created equates lack of control to a spiraling of events, and is not the reality of the events or of my life. Thinking that "If I had been there" and "I could have fixed it" are not true. I understand that we are only where we are and do what we do. We cannot control the past, the present or the future in the way we would like all the time and fantasies of how I would do better are neither logical or healthy. We do what we do relating to our reactions and mindset. There is no harm in preparing for the future, but doing so while dwelling on the past is wrong.

I believe both of the above also influence how I feel about safety. And that safety does not have to be a top priority anymore, but like above I can live my life without worrying. I believe that safety and trust go hand in hand for me and that stuck points and beliefs relating to trusting myself to not let others down are unfounded and that at I have not let others down, I can trust myself, and others and I am in a safe place both internally and externally. More than anything else, I know now that I am perfectly imperfect and I should trust myself to be a success and asset to myself, family, community and world.

We create a house around our souls. Some are more guarded than others. This house is framed with experiences and painted with our lives and fears. It is at home. A real home is not physical but where our minds feel at ease. There are dark rooms in this home, sure, but they are not necessarily the *Masque* containing a black room we can't avoid. We paint them how we want and flit in and out, the doors never close behind. There is always a way out of the rooms of despair and pain. And that is by groping from the dark corners using the frame as a guide. The doors always remain open for us.

Did I believe that when I wrote it? I do now. I moved on from those therapy sessions, back to my truck, back to my life, and began the hardest part of it all, keeping the thoughts and reactions what they needed to be.

NEW THERAPY
2019

Recently my wife and I made an appointment to see a therapist together. We had been experiencing difficulty in our marriage and with two little kids it seemed a little past time to seek help. Just that notion seemed weird to consider, but the idea of "we need help" rather than the "I do" that I was used to replaying in my mind over and over again seemed to jog loose some sense of urgency.

Sitting down in the psychologist's office, this new one, was odd to begin with. I was, and still am when I sit in there, wracked with anxiety of what Abbie is going to ask of me, what she is going to demand, what I need to talk to her about. Over the last thirteen years we have had a good life, a privileged life, one where the main sources of contention in many relationships were not necessary to bring up. We always had enough money with some to spare, we always were good partners and we love one another, but when kids came along, my attention waned, my anger flared over the slightest thing. I drank more, hoping to escape, and my thoughts of harming myself or killing myself roared back.

They would come at all hours. A sweeping discomfort and detachment hit me when I was already low. I watch in my head as my mind shows me a video of me putting two barrels of my shotgun in my mouth and using my toe or a stick. It cuts to after where everyone is weeping and the people, I wish understood me now have some concept of the pain that was going on in my mind. How each day is a waterfall. All the goodness flies over the edge to be smashed on the rocks and churned into nothingness before being spit out at the other end.

In the past, I would always hide those thoughts. I would go and work in my woodshop, grind and cut wood into shapes I wish my body could mold into. The geometry, planned, organized unlike my mind which seemed more like a jumble of wreckage, flotsam and jetsam drifting along a flooded moody river. I think one reason I did not tell my wife these things until recently is that I was afraid she would commit me, or realize that I was too much of a problem to handle and discard me. It's those irrational thoughts again. As silly as that seems now. She is orderly. Her father is an engineer, and she has that mindset. She is assertive and not aggressive or very passive, critical and confident, and that is something that I adore and am scared of.

After counseling where we addressed certain stuck points in our marriage that have bubbled freely under the surface for many years, we talk at home when the kids are down. It's one of those times where, in the kitchen, sitting high on the countertops, in the TV/workout room after a workout, on the bed, our feet bent high toward our pillows, heads down, honesty mixed with shame, I share, tell her my feelings, wait for what my mind has convinced me will happen, the fear, the anger, the judgment. None of them come, I get hugs instead, but I always worry.

I am open and honest with her about what my mind tells me and it is unbelievably liberating. How can someone hear what I tell her and still love me? How can I possibly tell her that I sometimes feel worried and stressed with the kids simply because they changed everything about our lives when I was so happy before them with time and freedom? On the same hand, how can I convince her that I love them and her more than my own life, more than the lives of every person on earth. How is it possible for her to understand that kind of cognitive dissonance when I don't? Perhaps she doesn't, perhaps she lies awake at night too.

When I tell her about that time with the bomb maker who attacked the Lt. and stuffed him in a shipping container only letting him out when the medics made us. How can I tell her about the night sleeping in a supposed death camp with open graves in the earth and the next day going to the doctor's house and torching all his equipment when he was simply saving whatever life came into his little clinic? Who did we kill as a byproduct of that crime? What about the hundred other moral crimes we committed every week? The flash grenades and pen flares thrown and shot at passing cars as retribution for a wave of anger at simply being there. All are crimes against the soul. That's what they are too. They are crimes against humanity. They were not illegal in war; they were sanctioned by our command. But, in the absence of a result coming from them, I know that they will fester in my mind and turn it like old milk. The actions begetting regret which in turn makes me stew over other actions and non-actions in my everyday life, forcing me to recount them half a million times before I let them go.

It's liberating to finally tell her of all the things I did and was witness to. I always was afraid that by making them real and speaking them they would take over me, but there is a certain power in being able to let them blow away like prayers on the wind. I don't think they will be going away any time soon, but I am able to let them buffer a little on her and she gets context while I get relief.

So, what is trauma as it pertains to war, or what I have learned? Without giving it some kind of mythical standing or metaphor like some many-headed snake, or something very Harry Potter-esque, I have come to know trauma as something much worse. At least when one sees a snake or monster, we are able to fight against it.

Years after leaving the Marines, perhaps four years or so after separation, I was studying English Literature at the University of Idaho and the VA rep, a man whom I came to love in my own way, a former Marine colonel, invited me to come to a dramatic reading the theatre department and volunteers were putting on. They were going to have a reading of various books and stories that showed war trauma and its aftermath on heroes of antiquity. Ajax, Achilles, Odysseus and others from Greek myths. A university psychologist would then have a talk about what PTSD actually was, and it promised to be a night of thoughtful consideration. I remember going alone. I don't know why my wife didn't come with me. Maybe I thought she couldn't handle it.

A jerk move like that sounds like me from a decade ago.

The readings were well done and thoughtful, the psychologist's talk was good and generalized to trauma and nothing more, but what was really disconcerting was that I found myself disagreeing, and finding some way to show that my trauma was manageable by myself, when he told me that I was not. Granted, he was talking to a room full of veterans and their families, and it was certainly in his best interests to convince us, but arrogant me sat there and shook my head thinking of how it was beatable with force of will.

Well, I went home and drank some whiskey and stayed up late thinking about why I thought I was able to fight my trauma on my own. I look at that thought now and shake my head I now know why Col. Button invited me, and why he put it on. I learned nothing from the experience for a while.

Those who killed themselves, or were consumed by problems were that way *because* they attempted to fight the mist of trauma on their own. They spent the rest of their lives flailing away at the darkness attempting to fight something that there really was no way they could beat with drink and thought. We can only beat the annihilation as a group, just like we started our war.

I have my box of military things at my house these days. I dredged it up from my parents' years ago and keep it in my garage, high in the rafters. Occasionally, I will go through it and wonder at the lack of letters, the lack of communication and that lack of internalization for what was going on around me. I have it all in there, the photo of me like Walt, my cammies and boots, a medic pack half used, and other artifacts from those years, but I don't find myself attached to them like I once was. I have a new life, and new purpose. I am able to look at those items as just that, items, nouns, things and ideas. That doesn't mean I have forgotten, far from it, but now I have something stronger to keep me going.

ACKNOWLEDGEMENTS

This book has been the effort of seven years of writing, editing, workshopping, crying, and agonizing. Anyone who has written a memoir, particularly about a traumatic time can attest, I am sure, that to do it one must live in that time and feeling over and over again, day after day at the computer, on walks, in conversation, everything about life conforms to the reliving of those experiences and the interpretation of them. During all of this, there were many who helped me through, and helped me understand what the events meant to my psyche.

I was very blessed to have gone through an MFA program. The MFA in Creative Nonfiction program at the University of Idaho gifted me with the foundations to write a memoir and more importantly, many incredible voices who carried me when the requirements of the project were seemingly impossible. First and foremost of that group was my professor and friend, Brandon R. Schrand, who led the year-long memoir workshop class which made me generate the first terrible drafts of this memoir. I remember having to show up to the first day of class in my first year with one-hundred and fifty pages written, and then handing them off to perfect strangers to dig into. Those strangers became close friends, as we were all reading each other's memoirs and learned the dark, happy, and sad secrets we carried together. Courtney Kersten, Jessica McDermott, and Jennifer Hawk were my first introductions to graduate student examples, and I could not have been blessed with anyone better. They became my model for how to write well, and how to critique with kindness. I could not have embarked on this project without those three and Brandon.

Additionally, in the same program, a whole host of mentors and friends have walked me through parts and stretches of this book, and the existential understanding and thought experiments over glasses of wine and pitchers of beer have been essential to me understanding the world how I do. Professors Kim Barnes, Anna Banks, Scott Slovic, Mary Clearman Blew, Ron McFarland, and many others guided me whether they know the extent or not. Because of them and their epochal presence, I have been able to understand a small amount of what is required of a writer of memoir. I cannot begin to thank them enough. Bryce Blankenship, a philosophy instructor at the University of Idaho and fellow wino walked me through many things over the years of writing related to how we see philosophy work in our lives, and his questioning and willingness to always talk me through an issue has been instrumental. Likewise, fellow writers Lauren Westerfield, Caitlin Hill, Sally Yazwinski, and many others deserve my thanks. My editor on this book, and fellow Marine JT Howard worked hard to provide me with thoughtful and unique insight to the problems and shortcomings of the narrative, I have been very lucky to have him on this project.

No amount of thanks would be complete without mentioning Ryan Mills outside of the narrative itself. Because of Ryan I am here. He not only has the knack of calling or texting me when I seem to need it most, but he took and continues to take his oath of service to the highest importance. He is a fellow fly-fisherman, the one who got me started woodworking, and is an all-around mentor and life saver. We could all do with a Ryan in our lives. Not only does he put up with my shit, but he does so with a laugh. I am very lucky to have him in my life.

Lastly, for these pages and for everything beyond them, I must thank my wife, Abbie. There is no thanks possible for the person who has not only put up with me over the years, but has done so gracefully and ever only with love. Abbie and my son and daughter have become my guides and constantly have helped me through this process. There is no thanks that is adequate for the love that she has given so freely. Abbie read many of these in the middle stages, once I became brave enough to share them with her, and she cried and thought and provided opinions and needed questions to help clarify pieces of this narrative for the non-veteran mind. She is the perfect editor and non-judgmental reader for my work.

MARINE SPEAK 101

AAV- Armored Amphibious Vehicle i.e. giant steel boxes that were great at attracting enemy fire.

Actual- a radio call sign for the officer in charge of a specific platoon

AO- Area of Operations

ASR-- Alternative Supply Route

Boots- New Marines, kids straight from infantry school

Battalion/Company/Platoon- A unit of Marines, usually a thousand strong. One Battalion usually has five companies (in the case of 2/7 they were HQ, Weapons, Golf, Echo, Fox companies). Every company is around two hundred men and contains five platoons of roughly forty men apiece.

Brig- Jail

CAX- Combined arms exercise that brings artillery, tanks, aircraft and grunts for a real show of force.

Click- the military name for a kilometer. Holds more of a 'cool' place in military terminology.

Flak- The body armor we wore as a jacket over our blouses.

FOB- Forward Operating Base

FRAGO-also known as Frag order. It is an impromptu order that transmits over the radio while already on patrol that usually modifies the mission to meet the needs of the overall commander's intent.

High and Tight- the most motivated haircut a Marine can get. It means high up on the head and no hair on the sides. I think it makes people's heads resemble a shiny penis.

HVT- High-Value Target

IED- Improvised Explosive Device

Jundies- Iraqi volunteer soldiers and police officers. Overall, they were worthless.

M-16 A4- Standard weapon of the Marine Infantry (The 'M' simply stands for model)

M-240 Golf- medium machine gun. This weapon was a crew served weapon that required the use of a gunner, assistant gunner, and ammo carrier. In a pinch, a big man can operate individually, and in the process, look like a real badass.

M-249 SAW- The Squad Automatic Weapon. Each squad carried two or three of these. One per fire team.

MCMAP- Marine Corps Martial Arts Program. It looks better than it is. The whole program focuses on submission and killing moves. I think it's pretty worthless until the later belts are achieved.

MCRD- Marine Corps Recruit Depot. West coast Marines train at MCRD while those east of the Mississippi go to Paris Island. West coast Marines are usually called "Hollywood Marines" by east coasters.

MOPP- stands for Mission Oriented Protective Posture. Physically, they are the suits we were supposed to wear in response to Saddam's suspected chemical weapon storage. We were supposed to have them, but never bothered to carry them.

Mustang- An officer who began in the enlisted ranks and went to college later to gain his commission.

MRE- Meal Ready to Eat...some say they have an unlimited shelf life...we tested that.

MSR- Main Supply Route

NCO-Non-Commissioned Officer. In the Marine Corps,

ranks of Corporal-Sergeant Major are non-commissioned officers.

PFT- Personal Fitness Test. This was a yearly requirement that all Marines participate. The score one receives on this test contributes toward his/her promotion.

POS- Position, another call the RO periodically gave to the main base.

PRC-119 A- the heavy-ass radio I carried on my back as an RO. It is a box around two feet wide, two feet tall and three inches thick. It weighs just enough to not be comfortable to carry over any distance.

PT- Physical Training

Ranger File- A column of men on patrol moving in a file one behind the other (with appropriate dispersion to keep from clustering up)

RO- Radio Operator

SitRep-- Situational Report the RO sends to the base when on patrol.

SOP- Standard Operating Procedure

Squad/Fireteam- the smallest units in the Marines. A platoon has three squads with around twelve men. Each squad has three fire teams of three to four men.

Thawb- often referred to as 'man dress,' this was the preferred clothing for men.

VBIED- Vehicle Borne Improvised Explosive Device, essentially a driver in a vehicle packed with explosives.

ABOUT ATMOSPHERE PRESS

Atmosphere Press is an independent, full-service publisher for excellent books in all genres and or all audiences. Learn more about what we do at atmospherepress.com.

We encourage you to check out some of Atmosphere's latest releases, which are available at Amazon.com and via order from your local bookstore:

Great Spirit of Yosemite: The Story of Chief Tenaya, nonfiction by Paul Edmondson

My Cemetery Friends: A Garden of Encounters at Mount Saint Mary in Queens, New York, nonfiction and poetry by Vincent J. Tomeo

Change in 4D, nonfiction by Wendy Wickham

Disruption Games: How to Thrive on Serial Failure, nonfiction by Trond Undheim

Eyeless Mind, nonfiction by Stephanie Duesing

A Blameless Walk, nonfiction by Charles Hopkins

The Horror of 1888, nonfiction by Betty Plombon

White Snake Diary, nonfiction by Jane P. Perry

From Rags to Rags, essays by Ellie Guzman

Giving Up the Ghost, essays by Tina Cabrera

Family Legends, Family Lies, nonfiction by Wendy Hoke

Shining in Infinity, a novel by Charles McIntyre

ABOUT THE AUTHOR

Paul Warmbier is a writer and teacher living in McMinnville, Oregon. His essays have appeared in various journals and outlets from *Allegory Ridge, Under the Sun, Watershed Review,* and others. Paul earned his MFA in Creative Non-Fiction from the University of Idaho. Currently, he is a High School Language Arts and Creative Writing teacher in a small town in Oregon.